To Joe and Connie — Special Friends
in the Lord. Thank you for ALL
you do and your Faithfulness
to our Lord and First Baptist.!!!
Psa. 118:24   Don and Judy R.

The Passion
of Jesus Christ

D1248771

Books by John Piper

God's Passion for His Glory

The Pleasures of God

Desiring God

The Dangerous Duty of Delight

Future Grace

A Hunger For God

Let the Nations Be Glad!

A Godward Life

A Godward Life, Book Two

Pierced by the Word

Seeing and Savoring Jesus Christ

The Legacy of Sovereign Joy

The Hidden Smile of God

The Roots of Endurance

The Misery of Job and the Mercy of God

The Innkeeper

The Prodigal's Sister

Recovering Biblical Manhood and Womanhood

What's the Difference?

The Justification of God

Counted Righteous in Christ

Brothers, We Are Not Professionals

The Supremacy of God in Preaching

Beyond the Bounds

Don't Waste Your Life

†HE PASSION OF JESUS CHRIST

Fifty Reasons Why He Came to Die

JOHN PIPER

CROSSWAY BOOKS

A DIVISION OF
GOOD NEWS PUBLISHERS
WHEATON, ILLINOIS

Cover design: Josh Dennis

Cover photo: Photonica

First printing, 2004

Printed in the United States of America

Library of Congress Cataloging-in-Publication Data
Piper, John, 1946-
 The Passion of Jesus Christ : fifty reasons why he came to die /
John Piper.
  p. cm.
 ISBN 1-58134-608-5 (TPB : alk. paper)
 1. Jesus Christ—Passion. I. Title.
BT431.3.P57 2004
232.96—dc22   2003026596

RRDC		14	13	12	11	10	09	08	07	06	05	04
16	15	14	13	12	11	10	9	8	7	6	5	4

TO
Jesus Christ

Despised and rejected by men;
a man of sorrows, and acquainted with grief . . .
we esteemed him stricken, smitten by God, and afflicted.
But he was wounded for our transgressions;
he was crushed for our iniquities;
upon him was the chastisement that brought us peace,
and with his stripes we are healed.

All we like sheep have gone astray;
we have turned every one to his own way;
and the LORD has laid on him the iniquity of us all.

He was oppressed, and he was afflicted,
yet he opened not his mouth;
like a lamb that is led to the slaughter,
and like a sheep that before its shearers is silent,
so he opened not his mouth. . . .

He was cut off out of the land of the living,
stricken for the transgression of my people. . . .
There was no deceit in his mouth.
Yet it was the will of the LORD to crush him;
he has put him to grief.

THE PROPHET ISAIAH
CHAPTER 53, VERSES 3-10

CONTENTS

The Christ, the Crucifixion, and the Concentration Camps

The most important question of the twenty-first century is: Why did Jesus Christ suffer so much? But we will never see this importance if we fail to go beyond human cause. The ultimate answer to the question, Who crucified Jesus? is: God did. It is a staggering thought. Jesus was his Son. And the suffering was unsurpassed. But the whole message of the Bible leads to this conclusion.

God Meant It for Good

The Hebrew prophet Isaiah said, "It was the will of the LORD to crush him; he has put him to grief" (Isaiah 53:10). The Christian New Testament says, "[God] did not spare his own Son but gave him up for us all" (Romans 8:32). "God put [Christ] forward . . . by his blood, to be received by faith" (Romans 3:25).

But how does this divine act relate to the horribly sinful actions of the men who killed Jesus? The answer given in the Bible is expressed in an early prayer: "There were gathered together against your holy servant Jesus . . . both Herod and Pontius Pilate, along with the Gentiles and the peoples of Israel, to do whatever your hand and your plan had predestined to take place" (Acts 4:27-28). The depth and scope of this divine sovereignty takes our breath away. But it is also the key to our salvation. God planned it, and by the means of wicked men, great good has come to the world. To paraphrase a word of the Jewish Torah: They meant it for evil, but God meant it for good (Genesis 50:20).

And since God meant it for good, we must move beyond the question of human cause to divine purpose. The central issue of Jesus' death is not the cause, but the purpose—the meaning. Man may have his reasons for wanting Jesus out of the way. But only God can design it for the good of the world. In fact, God's purposes for the world in the death of Jesus are unfathomable. I am scraping the surface in this little book as I introduce you to fifty of them. My aim is to let the Bible speak. This is where we hear the word of God. I hope that these pointers will set you on an endless quest to know more and more of God's great design in the death of his Son.

What Does the Word *Passion* Mean?

We associate at least four things with the word *passion*: sexual desire, zeal for a task, an oratorio by J. S. Bach, and the sufferings of Jesus Christ. The word comes from a Latin word meaning *suffering*. That is the way I am using it here—the sufferings and death of Jesus Christ. But it relates to all the other passions as well. It deepens sex, inspires music, and carries forward the greatest cause in the world.

How Was the Passion of Jesus Unique?

Why did the suffering and execution of a man who was convicted and condemned as a pretender to the throne of Rome unleash, in the next three centuries, a power to suffer and to love that transformed the Roman Empire, and to this day is shaping the world? The answer is that the passion of Jesus was absolutely unique, and his resurrection from the dead three days later was an act of God to vindicate what his death achieved.

His passion was unique because he was more than a mere human. Not less. He was, as the ancient Nicene Creed says, "very God of very God." This is the testimony of those who knew him and were inspired by him to explain who he is. The apostle John referred to Christ as "the Word" and wrote, "In the beginning was the Word, and the Word was with God, and the Word was God. He was in the beginning with God. All things were made through him, and without him was not any thing made that was made. . . . And the Word became flesh and dwelt among us, and we have seen his glory, glory as of the only Son from the Father, full of grace and truth" (John 1:1-3, 14).

Then add to his deity that he was utterly innocent in his suffering. Not just innocent of the charge of blasphemy, but of all sin. One of his closest disciples said, "He committed no sin, neither was deceit found in his mouth" (1 Peter 2:22). Then add to this uniqueness that he embraced his own death with absolute authority. One of the most stunning statements Jesus ever made was about his own death and resurrection: "I lay down my life that I may take it up again. No one takes it from me, but I lay it down of my own accord. I have authority to lay it down, and I have authority to take it up again. This charge I have received from my Father" (John 10:17-18). The controversy about who killed Jesus is marginal. He *chose* to die. His Father ordained it. He embraced it.

His Passion Was Vindicated by the Resurrection

Because of this unparalleled passion, God raised Jesus from the dead. It happened three days later. Early Sunday morning he rose from the dead. He appeared numerous times to his disciples for forty days before his ascension to heaven (Acts 1:3).

The disciples were slow to believe that it really happened. They were not gullible primitives. They were down-to-earth tradesmen. They knew people did not rise from the dead. At one point Jesus insisted on eating fish to prove to them that he was not a ghost (Luke 24:39-43). This was not the resuscitation of a corpse. It was the resurrection of the God-Man, into an indestructible new life. The early church acclaimed him Lord of heaven and earth. They said, "After making purification for sins, he sat down at the right hand of the Majesty on high" (Hebrews 1:3). Jesus had finished the work God gave him to do, and the resurrection was the proof that God was satisfied. This book is about what Jesus' passion accomplished for the world.

THE PASSION OF CHRIST AND THE PASSION OF AUSCHWITZ

It is a tragedy that the story of Christ's passion has produced anti-Semitism against Jews and crusading violence against Muslims. We Christians are ashamed of many of our ancestors who did not act in the spirit of Christ. No doubt there are traces of this plague in our own souls. But true Christianity—which is radically different from Western culture, and may not be found in many Christian churches—renounces the advance of religion by means of violence. "My kingdom is not of this world," Jesus said. "If my kingdom were of this world, my servants would have been fighting" (John 18:36). The way of the cross is the way of suffering. Christians are called to die, not kill, in order to show the world how they are loved by Christ.

Today this love humbly and boldly commends Christ, no matter what it costs, to all peoples as the only saving way to God. "Jesus said to him, 'I am the way, and the truth, and the life. No one comes to the Father except through me'" (John 14:6). But let it be crystal-clear: It is not Christian to humiliate or scorn or despise or persecute with prideful putdowns, or pogroms, or crusades, or concentration camps. These were and are, very simply and horribly, disobedience to Jesus Christ. Unlike many of his followers, he prayed from the cross, "Father, forgive them, for they know not what they do" (Luke 23:34).

The passion of Jesus Christ is the most important event in history, and the most explosive political and personal issue of the twenty-first century. The denial that Christ was crucified is like the denial of the Holocaust. For some it's simply too horrific to affirm. For others it's an elaborate conspiracy to coerce religious sympathy. But the deniers live in a historical dreamworld. Jesus Christ suffered unspeakably and died. So did Jews.

I am not the first to link Calvary and the concentration camps—the suffering of Jesus Christ and the suffering of Jewish people. In his heart-wrenching, innocence-shattering, mouth-shutting book *Night*, Elie Wiesel tells of his experience as a teenager with his father in the concentration camps of Auschwitz, Buna, and Buchenwald. There was always the threat of "the selection"—the taking away of the weak to be killed and burned in the ovens.

At one point—and only one—Wiesel links Calvary and the camps. He tells of an old rabbi, Akiba Dumer.

> Akiba Dumer left us, a victim of the selection. Lately, he had wandered among us, his eyes glazed, telling everyone of his weakness: "I can't go on . . . It's all over . . ." It was impossible to raise his morale. He didn't listen to what we told him. He could only repeat that all was over for him, that he could no longer keep up the struggle, that he had no strength left, nor faith. Suddenly his eyes would become blank, nothing but two open wounds, two pits of terror.[1]

Then Wiesel makes this provocative comment: "Poor Akiba Dumer, if he could have gone on believing in God, if he could have seen a proof of God in this Calvary, he would not have been taken by the selection."[2] I will not presume to put any words in

Elie Wiesel's mouth. I am not sure what he meant. But it presses the question: Why the link between Calvary and the concentration camp?

When I ask this question, I am not thinking of cause or blame. I am thinking of meaning and hope. Is there a way that Jewish suffering may find, not its cause, but its final meaning in the suffering of Jesus Christ? Is it possible to think, not of Christ's passion leading to Auschwitz, but of Auschwitz leading to an understanding of Christ's passion? Is the link between Calvary and the camps a link of unfathomable empathy? Perhaps only Jesus in the end can know what happened during the "one long night"[3] of Jewish suffering. And perhaps a generation of Jewish people, whose grandparents endured their own noxious crucifixion, will be able, as no others, to grasp what happened to the Son of God at Calvary. I leave it as a question. I do not know.

But this I know: Those ostensible "Christians" who built the camps never knew the love that moved Jesus Christ toward Calvary. They never knew the Christ, who instead of killing to save a culture, died to save the world. But there are some Christians—the true Christians—who have seen the meaning of the passion of Jesus Christ, and have been broken and humbled by his suffering. Could it be that these, perhaps better than many, might be able to see and, at least, begin to fathom the suffering of Jewish people?

What an irony that Christians have been anti-Semitic! Jesus and all his early followers were Jews. People from every group in Palestine were involved in his crucifixion (not just Jews), and people from every group opposed it (including Jews). God himself was the chief Actor in the death of his Son, so that the main question is not, Which humans brought about the death of Jesus? but, What did the death of Jesus bring about for humans—including Jews and Muslims and Buddhists and Hindus and nonreligious secularists—and all people everywhere?

When all is said and done, the most crucial question is: Why? Why did Christ suffer and die? Not why in the sense of *cause,* but why in the sense of *purpose.* What did Christ achieve by his passion? Why did he have to suffer so much? What great thing was happening on Calvary for the world?

That's what the rest of this book is about. I have gathered from the New Testament fifty reasons why Christ suffered and died. Not fifty causes, but fifty purposes. Infinitely more important than who killed Jesus is the question: *What did God achieve for sinners like us in sending his Son to die?* To that we now turn.

FIFTY REASONS WHY CHRIST SUFFERED AND DIED

TO ABSORB THE WRATH OF GOD

*Christ redeemed us from the curse of the law by becoming a
curse for us—for it is written,
"Cursed is everyone who is hanged on a tree."*

Galatians 3:13

*God put [Christ] forward as a propitiation by his blood,
to be received by faith. This was to show God's righteousness,
because in his divine forbearance he had passed over former sins.*

Romans 3:25

*In this is love, not that we have loved God but that he loved us
and sent his Son to be the propitiation for our sins.*

1 John 4:10

If God were not *just*, there would be no *demand* for his Son to
suffer and die. And if God were not *loving*, there would be no *willingness* for his Son to suffer and die. But God is both just and loving.
Therefore his love is willing to meet the demands of his justice.

God's law demanded, "You shall love the LORD your God with
all your heart and with all your soul and with all your might"
(Deuteronomy 6:5). But we have all loved other things more. This
is what sin is—dishonoring God by preferring other things over
him, and acting on those preferences. Therefore, the Bible says,
"All have sinned and fall short of the glory of God" (Romans
3:23). We glorify what we enjoy most. And it isn't God.

Therefore sin is not small, because it is not against a small Sovereign. The seriousness of an insult rises with the dignity of the one insulted. The Creator of the universe is infinitely worthy of respect and admiration and loyalty. Therefore, failure to love him is not trivial—it is treason. It defames God and destroys human happiness.

Since God is just, he does not sweep these crimes under the rug of the universe. He feels a holy wrath against them. They deserve to be punished, and he has made this clear: "For the wages of sin is death" (Romans 6:23). "The soul who sins shall die" (Ezekiel 18:4).

There is a holy curse hanging over all sin. Not to punish would be unjust. The demeaning of God would be endorsed. A lie would reign at the core of reality. Therefore, God says, "Cursed be everyone who does not abide by all things written in the Book of the Law, and do them" (Galatians 3:10; Deuteronomy 27:26).

But the love of God does not rest with the curse that hangs over all sinful humanity. He is not content to show wrath, no matter how holy it is. Therefore God sends his own Son to absorb his wrath and bear the curse for all who trust him. "Christ redeemed us from the curse of the law by becoming a curse for us" (Galatians 3:13).

This is the meaning of the word "propitiation" in the text quoted above (Romans 3:25). It refers to the removal of God's wrath by providing a substitute. The substitute is provided by God himself. The substitute, Jesus Christ, does not just cancel the wrath; he absorbs it and diverts it from us to himself. God's wrath is just, and it was spent, not withdrawn.

Let us not trifle with God or trivialize his love. We will never stand in awe of being loved by God until we reckon with the seriousness of our sin and the justice of his wrath against us. But when, by grace, we waken to our unworthiness, then we may look at the suffering and death of Christ and say, "In this is love, not that we have loved God but that he loved us and sent his Son to be the [wrath-absorbing] *propitiation* for our sins" (1 John 4:10).

TO PLEASE HIS HEAVENLY FATHER

Yet it was the will of the LORD to crush him;
he has put him to grief.

Isaiah 53:10

Christ loved us and gave himself up for us,
a fragrant offering and sacrifice to God.

Ephesians 5:2

Jesus did not wrestle his angry Father to the floor of heaven and take the whip out of his hand. He did not force him to be merciful to humanity. His death was not the begrudging consent of God to be lenient to sinners. No, what Jesus did when he suffered and died was the Father's idea. It was a breathtaking strategy, conceived even before creation, as God saw and planned the history of the world. That is why the Bible speaks of God's "purpose and grace, which he gave us in Christ Jesus before the ages began" (2 Timothy 1:9).

Already in the Jewish Scriptures the plan was unfolding. The prophet Isaiah foretold the sufferings of the Messiah, who was to take the place of sinners. He said that the Christ would be "smitten by God" in our place.

Surely he has borne our griefs and carried our sorrows; yet we esteemed him stricken, smitten by God, and afflicted. But he was wounded for our transgressions; he was crushed for our iniquities. . . . All we like sheep have gone astray; we have turned every one to his own way; and the LORD has laid on him the iniquity of us all. (Isaiah 53:4-6)

But what is most astonishing about this substitution of Christ for sinners is that it was God's idea. Christ did not intrude on God's plan to punish sinners. God planned for him to be there. One Old Testament prophet says, "It was the will of the LORD to crush him; he has put him to grief" (Isaiah 53:10).

This explains the paradox of the New Testament. On the one hand, the suffering of Christ is an outpouring of God's wrath because of sin. But on the other hand, Christ's suffering is a beautiful act of submission and obedience to the will of the Father. So Christ cried from the cross, "My God, my God, why have you forsaken me?" (Matthew 27:46). And yet the Bible says that the suffering of Christ was a fragrance to God. "Christ loved us and gave himself up for us, a fragrant offering and sacrifice to God" (Ephesians 5:2).

Oh, that we might worship the terrible wonder of the love of God! It is not sentimental. It is not simple. For our sake God did the impossible: He poured out his wrath on his own Son—the one whose submission made him infinitely unworthy to receive it. Yet the Son's very willingness to receive it was precious in God's sight. The wrath-bearer was infinitely loved.

To Learn Obedience and Be Perfected

Although he was a son, he learned obedience
through what he suffered.

Hebrews 5:8

For it was fitting that he, for whom and by whom all things exist,
in bringing many sons to glory,
should make the founder of their salvation
perfect through suffering.

Hebrews 2:10

The very book in the Bible that says Christ "learned obedience" through suffering, and that he was "made perfect" through suffering, also says that he was "without sin." "In every respect [Christ] has been tempted as we are, *yet without sin*" (Hebrews 4:15).

This is the consistent teaching of the Bible. Christ was sinless. Although he was the divine Son of God, he was really human, with all our temptations and appetites and physical weaknesses. There was hunger (Matthew 21:18) and anger and grief (Mark 3:5) and pain (Matthew 17:12). But his heart was perfectly in love with God, and he acted consistently with that love: "He committed no sin, neither was deceit found in his mouth" (1 Peter 2:22).

Therefore, when the Bible says that Jesus "learned obedience through what he suffered," it doesn't mean that he learned to stop disobeying. It means that with each new trial he learned in practice—and in pain—what it means to obey. When it says that he was "made perfect through suffering," it doesn't mean that he was gradually getting rid of defects. It means that he was gradually fulfilling the perfect righteousness that he had to have in order to save us.

That's what he said at his baptism. He didn't need to be baptized because he was a sinner. Rather, he explained to John the Baptist, "Thus it is fitting for us to fulfill all righteousness" (Matthew 3:15).

The point is this: *If the Son of God had gone from incarnation to the cross without a life of temptation and pain to test his righteousness and his love, he would not be a suitable Savior for fallen man.* His suffering not only absorbed the wrath of God. It also fulfilled his true humanity and made him able to call us brothers and sisters (Hebrews 2:17).

To Achieve His Own Resurrection from the Dead

*Now may the God of peace who brought again from the dead
our Lord Jesus, the great shepherd of the sheep,
by the blood of the eternal covenant,
equip you with everything good that you may do his will.*

Hebrews 13:20-21

The death of Christ did not merely precede his resurrection—
it was the price that obtained it. That's why Hebrews 13:20
says that God brought him from the dead "by the blood of the
eternal covenant."

The "blood of the . . . covenant" is the blood of Jesus. As he
said, "This is my blood of the covenant" (Matthew 26:28). When
the Bible speaks of the blood of Jesus, it refers to his death. No
salvation would be accomplished by the mere bleeding of Jesus.
His bleeding *to death* is what makes his blood-shedding crucial.

Now what is the relationship between this shedding of Jesus'
blood and the resurrection? The Bible says he was raised not just
after the blood-shedding, but *by* it. This means that what the death
of Christ accomplished was so full and so perfect that the resurrection was the *reward* and *vindication* of Christ's achievement in
death.

The wrath of God was satisfied with the suffering and death

of Jesus. The holy curse against sin was fully absorbed. The obedience of Christ was completed to the fullest measure. The price of forgiveness was totally paid. The righteousness of God was completely vindicated. All that was left to accomplish was the public declaration of God's endorsement. This he gave by raising Jesus from the dead.

When the Bible says, "If Christ has not been raised, your faith is futile and you are still in your sins" (1 Corinthians 15:17), the point is not that the resurrection is the price paid for our sins. The point is that the resurrection proves that the death of Jesus is an all-sufficient price. If Jesus did not rise from the dead, then his death was a failure, God did not vindicate his sin-bearing achievement, and we are still in our sins.

But in fact "Christ was raised from the dead by the glory of the Father" (Romans 6:4). The success of his suffering and death was vindicated. And if we put our trust in Christ, we are *not* still in our sins. For "*by* the blood of the eternal covenant," the Great Shepherd has been raised and lives forever.

To Show the Wealth of God's Love and Grace for Sinners

One will scarcely die for a righteous person—
though perhaps for a good person one would dare even to die—
but God shows his love for us in that while we were still sinners,
Christ died for us.

Romans 5:7-8

For God so loved the world, that he gave his only Son,
that whoever believes in him should not perish but have eternal life.

John 3:16

In him we have redemption through his blood,
the forgiveness of our trespasses,
according to the riches of his grace.

Ephesians 1:7

The measure of God's love for us is shown by two things. One is the degree of his sacrifice in saving us from the penalty of our sin. The other is the degree of unworthiness that we had when he saved us.

We can hear the measure of his sacrifice in the words, "He gave his only son" (John 3:16). We also hear it in the word *Christ*. This is a name based on the Greek title *Christos*, or "Anointed One," or "Messiah." It is a term of great dignity. The Messiah was to be the King of Israel. He would conquer the

Romans and bring peace and security to Israel. Thus the person whom God sent to save sinners was his own divine Son, his *only* Son, and the Anointed King of Israel—indeed the king of the world (Isaiah 9:6-7).

When we add to this consideration the horrific death by crucifixion that Christ endured, it becomes clear that the sacrifice the Father and the Son made was indescribably great—even infinite, when you consider the distance between the divine and the human. But God chose to make this sacrifice to save us.

The measure of his love for us increases still more when we consider our unworthiness. "Perhaps for a good person one would dare even to die—but God shows his love for us in that *while we were still sinners*, Christ died for us" (Romans 5:7-8). We deserved divine punishment, not divine sacrifice.

I have heard it said, "God didn't die for frogs. So he was responding to our value as humans." This turns grace on its head. We are *worse* off than frogs. They have not sinned. They have not rebelled and treated God with the contempt of being inconsequential in their lives. God did not have to die for frogs. They aren't bad enough. We are. Our debt is so great, only a divine sacrifice could pay it.

There is only one explanation for God's sacrifice for us. It is not us. It is "the riches of his grace" (Ephesians 1:7). It is all free. It is not a response to our worth. It is the overflow of his infinite worth. In fact, that is what divine love is in the end: a passion to enthrall undeserving sinners, at great cost, with what will make us supremely happy forever, namely, his infinite beauty.

TO SHOW HIS OWN LOVE
FOR US

Christ loved us and gave himself up for us,
a fragrant offering and sacrifice to God.

EPHESIANS 5:2

Christ loved the church and gave himself up for her.

EPHESIANS 5:25

[He] loved me and gave himself for me.

GALATIANS 2:20

The death of Christ is not only the demonstration of *God's* love (John 3:16), it is also the supreme expression of *Christ's own* love for all who receive it as their treasure. The early witnesses who suffered most for being Christians were captured by this fact: Christ "loved me and gave himself for me" (Galatians 2:20). They took the self-giving act of Christ's sacrifice very personally. They said, "He loved *me*. He gave himself for *me*."

Surely this is the way we should understand the sufferings and death of Christ. They have to do with me. They are about Christ's love for me personally. It is *my* sin that cuts me off from God, not sin in general. It is *my* hard-heartedness and spiritual numbness that demean the worth of Christ. I am lost and perishing. When it comes to salvation, I have forfeited all claim on justice. All I can do is plead for mercy.

Then I see Christ suffering and dying. For whom? It says,

"Christ loved the *church* and gave himself up for *her*" (Ephesians 5:25). "Greater love has no one than this, that someone lays down his life for *his friends*" (John 15:13). "The Son of Man came not to be served but to serve, and to give his life as a ransom for *many*" (Matthew 20:28).

And I ask, Am I among the "many"? Can I be one of his "friends"? May I belong to the "church"? And I hear the answer, "Believe in the Lord Jesus, and you will be saved" (Acts 16:31). "Everyone who calls on the name of the Lord will be saved" (Romans 10:13). "Everyone who believes in him receives forgiveness of sins through his name" (Acts 10:43). "To all who did receive him, who believed in his name, he gave the right to become children of God" (John 1:12). "Whoever believes in him should not perish but have eternal life" (John 3:16).

My heart is swayed, and I embrace the beauty and bounty of Christ as my treasure. And there flows into my heart this great reality—the love of Christ for me. So I say with those early witnesses, "He loved me and gave himself for me."

And what do I mean? I mean that he paid the highest price possible to give me the greatest gift possible. And what is that? It is the gift he prayed for at the end of his life: "Father, I desire that they also, whom you have given me, may be with me where I am, to see my glory" (John 17:24). In his suffering and death "we have seen his glory, glory as of the only Son from the Father, full of grace and truth" (John 1:14). We have seen enough to capture us for his cause. But the best is yet to come. He died to secure this for us. That is the love of Christ.

To Cancel the Legal Demands of the Law Against Us

And you, who were dead in your trespasses . . .
God made alive together with him,
having forgiven us all our trespasses,
by canceling the record of debt that stood
against us with its legal demands.
This he set aside, nailing it to the cross.

Colossians 2:13

What a folly it is to think that our good deeds may one day outweigh our bad deeds. It is folly for two reasons.

First, *it is not true.* Even our good deeds are defective, because we don't honor God in the way we do them. Do we do our good deeds in joyful dependence on God with a view to making known his supreme worth? Do we fulfill the overarching command to serve people "by the strength that God supplies—in order that in everything God may be glorified through Jesus Christ" (1 Peter 4:11)?

What then shall we say in response to God's word, "Whatever does not proceed from faith is sin" (Romans 14:23)? I think we shall say nothing. "Whatever the law says it speaks . . . so that every mouth may be stopped" (Romans 3:19). We will say nothing. It is folly to think that our good deeds will outweigh our bad deeds before God. Without Christ-exalting faith, our deeds will signify nothing but rebellion.

The second reason it is folly to hope in good deeds is that *this is not the way God saves*. If we are saved from the consequences of our bad deeds, it will not be because they weighed less than our good deeds. It will be because the "record of [our] debt" in heaven has been nailed to the cross of Christ. God has a totally different way of saving sinners than by weighing their deeds. There is no hope in our deeds. There is only hope in the suffering and death of Christ.

There is no salvation by balancing the records. There is only salvation by canceling records. The record of our bad deeds (including our defective good deeds), along with the just penalties that each deserves, must be blotted out—not balanced. This is what Christ suffered and died to accomplish.

The cancellation happened when the record of our deeds was "nailed to the cross" (Colossians 2:13). How was this damning record nailed to the cross? Parchment was not nailed to the cross. Christ was. So Christ became my damning record of bad (and good) deeds. He endured my damnation. He put my salvation on a totally different footing. He is my only hope. And faith in him is my only way to God.

To Become a Ransom for Many

*The Son of Man came not to be served but to serve,
and to give his life as a ransom for many.*

Mark 10:45

There is no thought in the Bible that Satan had to be paid off to let sinners be saved. What happened to Satan when Christ died was not payment, but defeat. The Son of God became human so "that through death he might destroy the one who has the power of death, that is, the devil" (Hebrews 2:14). There was no negotiation.

When Jesus says that he came "to give his life as a ransom," the focus is not on who gets the payment. The focus is on his own life as the payment, and on his freedom in serving rather than being served, and on the "many" who will benefit from the payment he makes.

If we ask who received the ransom, the biblical answer would surely be God. The Bible says that Christ "gave himself up for us, [an] . . . offering . . . *to God*" (Ephesians 5:2). Christ "offered himself without blemish *to God*" (Hebrews 9:14). The whole need for a substitute to die on our behalf is because we have sinned against *God* and fallen short of the glory of *God* (Romans 3:23). And because of our sin, "the whole world [is] held accountable to *God*" (Romans 3:19). So when Christ gives himself as a ransom for us, the Bible says that we are freed from the condemnation of God. "There is therefore now no condemnation for those who are in Christ Jesus" (Romans 8:1). The ultimate captivity from which we need release is the final "judgment of *God*" (Romans 2:2; Revelation 14:7).

The ransom price of this release from God's condemnation is the life of Christ. Not just his life lived, but his life given up in death. Jesus said repeatedly to his disciples, "The Son of Man is going to be delivered into the hands of men, and they will kill him" (Mark 9:31). In fact, one of the reasons Jesus loved to call himself "the Son of Man" (over sixty-five times in the Gospels) was that it had the ring of mortality about it. Men can die. That's why he had to be one. The ransom could only be paid by the Son of Man, because the ransom was a life given up in death.

The price was not coerced from him. That's the point of saying, "The Son of Man came not to be served but to serve." He needed no service from us. He was the giver, not the receiver. "No one takes [my life] from me, but I lay it down of my own accord" (John 10:18). The price was paid freely; it was not forced. Which brings us again to his love. He freely chose to rescue us at the cost of his life.

How many did Christ effectively ransom from sin? He said that he came "to give his life as a ransom *for many*." Yet not everyone will be ransomed from the wrath of God. But the *offer* is for everyone. "There is one mediator between God and men, the man Christ Jesus, who gave himself as a ransom *for all*" (1 Timothy 2:5-6). No one is excluded from this salvation who embraces the treasure of the ransoming Christ.

FOR THE FORGIVENESS OF OUR SINS

*In him we have redemption through his blood,
the forgiveness of our trespasses.*

E p h e s i a n s   1 : 7

*This is my blood of the covenant,
which is poured out for many
for the forgiveness of sins.*

M a t t h e w   2 6 : 2 8

When we forgive a debt or an offense or an injury, we don't require a payment for settlement. That would be the opposite of forgiveness. If repayment is made to us for what we lost, there is no need for forgiveness. We have our due.

Forgiveness assumes grace. If I am injured by you, grace lets it go. I don't sue you. I forgive you. Grace gives what someone doesn't deserve. That's why *forgiveness* has the word *give* in it. For*give*ness is not "*get*ting" even. It is giving away the right to get even.

That is what God does to us when we trust Christ: "Everyone who believes in him receives forgiveness of sins through his name" (Acts 10:43). If we believe in Christ, God no longer holds our sins against us. This is God's own testimony in the Bible: "I, I am he who wipes out your transgressions for my own sake" (Isaiah 43:25). "As far as the east is from the west, so far does he remove our transgressions from us" (Psalm 103:12).

But this raises a problem. We all know that forgiveness is not enough. We may only see it clearly when the injury is great—like murder or rape. Neither society nor the universe can hold together if judges (or God) simply say to every murderer and rapist, "Are you sorry? Okay. The state forgives you. You may go." In cases like these we see that while a victim may have a forgiving spirit, the state cannot forsake justice.

So it is with God's justice. All sin is serious, because it is against God (see chapter 1). He is the one whose glory is injured when we ignore or disobey or blaspheme him. His justice will no more allow him simply to set us free than a human judge can cancel all the debts that criminals owe to society. The injury done to God's glory by our sin must be repaired so that in justice his glory shines more brightly. And if we criminals are to go free and be forgiven, there must be some dramatic demonstration that the honor of God is upheld even though former blasphemers are being set free.

That is why Christ suffered and died. "In him we have redemption *through his blood*, the forgiveness of our trespasses" (Ephesians 1:7). Forgiveness costs us nothing. All our costly obedience is the fruit, not the root, of being forgiven. That's why we call it grace. But it cost Jesus his life. That is why we call it just. Oh, how precious is the news that God does not hold our sins against us! And how beautiful is Christ, whose blood made it right for God to do this.

TO PROVIDE THE BASIS FOR OUR JUSTIFICATION

We have now been justified by his blood.

ROMANS 5:9

[We] are justified by his grace as a gift, through the redemption that is in Christ Jesus.

ROMANS 3:24

We hold that one is justified by faith apart from works of the law.

ROMANS 3:28

Being justified before God and being forgiven by God are not identical. To be justified in a courtroom is not the same as being forgiven. Being forgiven implies that I am guilty and my crime is not counted. Being justified implies that I have been tried and found innocent. My claim is just. I am vindicated. The *judge* says, "Not guilty."

Justifying is a legal act. It means declaring someone to be just. It is a verdict. The verdict of justification does not *make* a person just. It *declares* a person just. It is based on someone actually being just. We can see this most clearly when the Bible tells us that, in response to Jesus' teaching, the people "justified" *God* (Luke 7:29). This does not mean they *made* God just (since he already was). It means they declared God to be just.

The moral change we undergo when we trust Christ is not justification. The Bible usually calls that sanctification—the process of becoming good. Justification is not that process. It is not a process at all. It is a declaration that happens in a moment. A verdict: Just! Righteous!

The ordinary way to be justified in a human court is to keep the law. In that case the jury and the judge simply declare what is true of you: You kept the law. They justify you. But in the courtroom of God, we have *not* kept the law. Therefore, justification, on ordinary terms, is hopeless. The Bible even says, "He who justifies the wicked [is] an abomination to the LORD" (Proverbs 17:15). And yet, amazingly, because of Christ, it also says God "justifies the ungodly" who trust in his grace (Romans 4:5). God does what looks abominable.

Why is it not abominable? Or, as the Bible puts it, how can God "be just *and* the justifier of the one who [simply!] has faith in Jesus" (Romans 3:26)? It is not abominable for God to justify the ungodly who trust him, for two reasons. One is that *Christ shed his blood to cancel the guilt of our crime.* So it says, "We have now been justified *by his blood*" (Romans 5:9). But that is only the removal of guilt. That does not declare us righteous. Canceling our failures to keep the law is not the same as declaring us to be a law-keeper. When a teacher cancels from the record an exam that got an F, it's not the same as declaring it an A. If the bank were to forgive me the debts on my account, that would not be the same as declaring me rich. So also, canceling our sins is not the same as declaring us righteous. The cancellation must happen. That is essential to justification. But there is more. There is another reason why it is not abominable for God to justify the ungodly by faith. For that we turn to the next chapter.

To Complete the Obedience That Becomes Our Righteousness

Being found in human form, he humbled himself by becoming obedient to the point of death, even death on a cross.

Philippians 2:8

For as by the one man's disobedience the many were made sinners, so by the one man's obedience the many will be made righteous.

Romans 5:19

For our sake he made him to be sin who knew no sin, so that in him we might become the righteousness of God.

2 Corinthians 5:21

. . . not having a righteousness of my own that comes from the law, but that which comes through faith in Christ.

Philippians 3:9

Justification is not merely the cancellation of my unrighteousness. It is also the imputation of Christ's righteousness to me. I do not have a righteousness that commends me to God. My claim before God is this: "not having a righteousness of my own that comes from the law, but that which comes through faith in Christ" (Philippians 3:9).

This is Christ's righteousness. It is imputed to me. That means Christ fulfilled all righteousness perfectly; and then that righteousness was reckoned to be mine, when I trusted in him. I was counted righteous. God looked on Christ's perfect righteousness, and he declared me to be righteous with the righteousness of Christ.

So there are two reasons why it is not abominable for God to justify the ungodly (Romans 4:5). First, *the death of Christ paid the debt of our unrighteousness* (see the previous chapter). Second, *the obedience of Christ provided the righteousness we needed to be justified in God's court.* The demands of God for entrance into eternal life are not merely that our unrighteousness be canceled, but that our perfect righteousness be established.

The suffering and death of Christ is the basis of both. His suffering is the suffering that our unrighteousness deserved. "He was wounded for our transgressions; he was crushed for our iniquities" (Isaiah 53:5). But his suffering and death were also the climax and completion of the obedience that became the basis of our justification. He was "obedient to the point of death, even death on a cross" (Philippians 2:8). His death was the pinnacle of his obedience. This is what the Bible refers to when it says, "By the one man's obedience the many will be made righteous" (Romans 5:19).

Therefore, Christ's death became the basis of our pardon and our perfection. "For our sake [God] made him to be sin who knew no sin, so that in him we might become the righteousness of God" (2 Corinthians 5:21). What does it mean that God made the sinless Christ to be sin? It means our sin was imputed to him, and thus he became our pardon. And what does it mean that we (who *are* sinners) become the righteousness of God in Christ? It means, similarly, that Christ's righteousness is imputed to us, and thus he became our perfection.

May Christ be honored for his whole achievement in suffering and dying! Both the work of pardoning our sin, and the work of providing our righteousness. Let us admire him and treasure him and trust him for this great achievement.

To Take Away Our Condemnation

*Who is to condemn? Christ Jesus is the one who died—
more than that, who was raised—who is at the right hand
of God, who indeed is interceding for us.*

Romans 8:34

The great conclusion to the suffering and death of Christ is this: "There is therefore now no condemnation for those who are in Christ Jesus" (Romans 8:1). To be "in Christ" means to be in relationship to him by faith. Faith in Christ unites us to Christ so that his death becomes our death and his perfection becomes our perfection. Christ becomes our punishment (which we don't have to bear) and our perfection (which we cannot perform).

Faith is not the ground of our acceptance with God. Christ alone is. Faith unites us to Christ so that his righteousness is counted as ours. "We know that a person is not justified by works of the law but through faith in Jesus Christ, so we also have believed in Christ Jesus, in order to be justified by faith in Christ and not by works of the law, because by works of the law no one will be justified" (Galatians 2:16). Being "justified by faith" and being "justified . . . in Christ" (Galatians 2:17) are parallel terms. We are in Christ by faith, and therefore justified.

When the question is asked, "Who is to condemn?" the answer is assumed. No one! Then the basis is declared: "Christ Jesus is the one who died!" The death of Christ secures our freedom from condemnation. It is as sure that we cannot be condemned as it is sure that Christ died. There is no double jeopardy in God's court. We will not be condemned twice for the same offenses. Christ has died once for our sins. We will not be condemned for them. Condemnation is gone not because there isn't any, but because it has already happened.

But what about condemnation by the world? Is that not an answer to the question, "Who is to condemn?" Aren't Christians condemned by the world? There have been many martyrs. The answer is that no one can condemn us *successfully*. Charges can be brought, but none will stick in the end. "Who shall bring any charge against God's elect? It is God who justifies" (Romans 8:33). It's the same as when the Bible asks, "Who shall separate us from the love of Christ? Shall tribulation, or distress, or persecution, or famine, or nakedness, or danger, or sword?" (Romans 8:35). The answer is not that these things don't happen to Christians. The answer is: "In all these things we are more than conquerors through him who loved us" (Romans 8:37).

The world will bring its condemnation. They may even put their sword behind it. But we know that the highest court has already ruled in our favor. "If God is for us, who can be against us?" (Romans 8:31). No one successfully. If they reject us, he accepts us. If they hate us, he loves us. If they imprison us, he sets our spirits free. If they afflict us, he refines us by the fire. If they kill us, he makes it a passage to paradise. They cannot defeat us. Christ has died. Christ is risen. We are alive in him. And in him there is no condemnation. We are forgiven, and we are righteous. "And the righteous are bold as a lion" (Proverbs 28:1).

TO ABOLISH CIRCUMCISION AND ALL RITUALS AS THE BASIS OF SALVATION

But if I, brothers, still preach circumcision . . .
the offense of the cross has been removed.

Galatians 5:11

It is those who want to make a good showing in the flesh
who would force you to be circumcised, and only in order that
they may not be persecuted for the cross of Christ.

Galatians 6:12

The place of circumcision was a huge controversy in the early church. It had a long, respected, biblical place ever since God commanded it in Genesis 17:10. Christ was a Jew. All his twelve apostles were Jews. Almost all the first converts to Christianity were Jews. The Jewish Scriptures were (and are) part of the Bible of the Christian church. It is not surprising that Jewish rituals would come over into the Christian church.

They came. And with them came controversy. The message of Christ was spreading to non-Jewish cities like Antioch of Syria. Gentiles were believing on Christ. The question became urgent: How did the central truth of the gospel relate to rituals like circumcision? How did rituals relate to the gospel of Christ—the news that, if you believe on him your sins are forgiven, and you are justified before God? God is for you. You have eternal life.

Throughout the Gentile world the apostles were preaching forgiveness and justification by faith alone. Peter preached: "To [Christ] all the prophets bear witness that everyone who believes in him receives *forgiveness of sins* through his name" (Acts 10:43). Paul preached: "Let it be known to you therefore, brothers, that . . . by him everyone who believes is *justified* from everything from which you could not be *justified* by the law of Moses" (Acts 13:38-39, author's translation).

But what about circumcision? Some in Jerusalem thought it was essential. Antioch became the flash point for the controversy. "Men came down from Judea and were teaching the brothers, 'Unless you are circumcised . . . you cannot be saved'" (Acts 15:1). A council was called, and the matter was debated.

> *Some . . . rose up and said, "It is necessary to circumcise them and to order them to keep the law of Moses." . . . Peter stood up and said to them, "Brothers, you know that . . . God made a choice among you, that by my mouth the Gentiles should hear the word of the gospel and believe . . . why are you putting God to the test by placing a yoke on the neck of the disciples that neither our fathers nor we have been able to bear? But we believe that we will be saved through the grace of the Lord Jesus, just as they will." And all the assembly fell silent. (Acts 15:5-12)*

Nobody saw to the bottom of the issue more clearly than the apostle Paul. The very meaning of the suffering and death of Christ was at stake. Was faith in Christ enough to put us right with God? Or was circumcision necessary too? The answer was clear. If Paul preached circumcision, "the offense of the cross has been removed" (Galatians 5:11). The cross means freedom from the enslavement of ritual. "For freedom Christ has set us free; stand firm therefore, and do not submit again to a yoke of slavery" (Galatians 5:1).

To Bring Us to Faith and Keep Us Faithful

This is my blood of the covenant, which is poured out for many.
Mark 14:24

I will make with them an everlasting covenant. . . .
And I will put the fear of me in their hearts,
that they may not turn from me.
Jeremiah 32:40

The Bible speaks of an "old covenant" and a "new covenant." The term *covenant* refers to a solemn, binding agreement between two parties carrying obligations for both sides and enforced by an oath. In the Bible the covenants God makes with man are initiated by himself. He sets the terms. His obligations are determined by his own purposes.

The "old covenant" refers to the arrangement God established with Israel in the law of Moses. Its weakness was that it was not accompanied by spiritual transformation. Therefore it was not obeyed and did not bring life. It was written with letters on stone, not with the Spirit on the heart. The prophets promised a "new covenant" that would be different. It would be "not of the letter but of the Spirit. For the letter kills, but the Spirit gives life" (2 Corinthians 3:6).

The new covenant is radically more effective than the old. It is enacted on the foundation of Jesus' suffering and death. "He is the mediator of a new covenant" (Hebrews 9:15). Jesus said that his blood was the "blood of the covenant, which is poured out for many" (Mark 14:24). This means that the blood of Jesus purchased the power and the promises of the new covenant. It is supremely effective because Christ died to make it so.

What then are the terms of the covenant that he infallibly secured by his blood? The prophet Jeremiah describes some of them: "I will make a new covenant . . . this is the covenant that I will make . . . I will put my law within them, and I will write it on their hearts. . . . For I will forgive their iniquity, and I will remember their sin no more" (Jeremiah 31:31-34). The suffering and death of Christ guarantees the inner change of his people (the law written on their hearts) and the forgiveness of their sins.

To guarantee that this covenant will not fail, Christ takes the initiative to create the faith and secure the faithfulness of his people. He brings a new-covenant people into being by writing the law not just on stone, but on the heart. In contrast with the "letter" on stone, he says "the Spirit gives life" (2 Corinthians 3:6). "When we were dead in our trespasses, [God] made us alive together with Christ" (Ephesians 2:5). This is the spiritual life that enables us to see and believe in the glory of Christ. This miracle creates the new-covenant people. It is sure and certain because Christ bought it with his own blood.

And the miracle is not only the creation of our faith, but the securing of our faithfulness. "I will make with them an everlasting covenant. . . . I will put the fear of me in their hearts, that they may not turn from me" (Jeremiah 32:40). When Christ died, he secured for his people not only new hearts but new security. He will not let them turn from him. He will keep them. They will persevere. The blood of the covenant guarantees it.

To Make Us Holy, Blameless, and Perfect

For by a single offering he has perfected for all time those who are being sanctified.

Hebrews 10:14

He has now reconciled [you] in his body of flesh by his death, in order to present you holy and blameless and above reproach before him.

Colossians 1:22

Cleanse out the old leaven that you may be a new lump, as you really are unleavened. For Christ, our Passover lamb, has been sacrificed.

1 Corinthians 5:7

One of the greatest heartaches in the Christian life is the slowness of our change. We hear the summons of God to love him with all our heart and soul and mind and strength (Mark 12:30). But do we ever rise to that totality of affection and devotion? We cry out regularly with the apostle Paul, "Wretched man that I am! Who will deliver me from this body of death?" (Romans 7:24). We groan even as we take fresh resolves: "Not that I have already obtained this or am already perfect, but I press on to make it my own, because Christ Jesus has made me his own" (Philippians 3:12).

That very statement is the key to endurance and joy. "Christ Jesus has made me his own." All my reaching and yearning and striving is not to belong to Christ (which has already happened), but to complete what is lacking in my likeness to him.

One of the greatest sources of joy and endurance for the Christian is knowing that in the imperfection of our progress we have already been perfected—and that this is owing to the suffering and death of Christ. "For by a single offering [namely, himself!] he has perfected for all time those who are being sanctified" (Hebrews 10:14). This is amazing! In the same sentence he says we are "being sanctified" and we are already "perfected."

Being sanctified means that we are imperfect and in process. We are becoming holy—but are not yet fully holy. And it is precisely these—and only these—who are already perfected. The joyful encouragement here is that the evidence of our perfection before God is not our experienced perfection, but our experienced progress. The good news is that being on the way is proof that we have arrived.

The Bible pictures this again in the old language of dough and leaven (yeast). In the picture, leaven is evil. We are the lump of dough. It says, "Cleanse out the old leaven that you may be a new lump, as you really are unleavened. For Christ, our Passover lamb, has been sacrificed" (1 Corinthians 5:7). Christians are "unleavened." There is no leaven—no evil. We are perfected. For this reason we are to "cleanse out the old leaven." We have been made unleavened in Christ. So we should now become unleavened in practice. In other words, we should become what we are.

The basis of all this? "For Christ, our Passover lamb, has been sacrificed." The suffering of Christ secures our perfection so firmly that it is already now a reality. Therefore, we fight against our sin not simply to *become* perfect, but because we *are*. The death of Jesus is the key to battling our imperfections on the firm foundation of our perfection.

TO GIVE US A CLEAR CONSCIENCE

How much more will the blood of Christ,
who through the eternal Spirit offered himself
without blemish to God, purify our conscience from
dead works to serve the living God.

Hebrews 9:14

Some things never change. The problem of a dirty conscience is as old as Adam and Eve. As soon as they sinned, their conscience was defiled. Their sense of guilt was ruinous. It ruined their relationship with God—they hid from him. It ruined their relation to each other—they blamed. It ruined their peace with themselves—for the first time they saw themselves and felt shame.

All through the Old Testament, conscience was an issue. But the animal sacrifices themselves could not cleanse the conscience. "Gifts and sacrifices are offered that cannot perfect the conscience of the worshiper, but deal only with food and drink and various washings, regulations for the body imposed until the time of reformation" (Hebrews 9:9-10). As a foreshadowing of Christ, God counted the blood of the animals as sufficient for cleansing the flesh—the ceremonial uncleanness, but not the conscience.

No animal blood could cleanse the conscience. They knew it (see Isaiah 53 and Psalm 51). And we know it. So a new high priest comes—Jesus the Son of God—with a better sacrifice: himself.

"How much more will the blood of Christ, who through the eternal Spirit offered himself without blemish to God, purify our conscience from dead works to serve the living God" (Hebrews 9:14). The animal sacrifices foreshadowed the final sacrifice of God's Son, and the death of the Son reaches back to cover all the sins of God's people in the old time period, and forward to cover all the sins of God's people in the new time period.

So here we are in the modern age—the age of science, Internet, organ transplants, instant messaging, cell phones—and our problem is fundamentally the same as always: Our conscience condemns us. We don't feel good enough to come to God. And no matter how distorted our consciences are, this much is true: We are not good enough to come to him.

We can cut ourselves, or throw our children in the sacred river, or give a million dollars to the United Way, or serve in a soup kitchen on Thanksgiving, or perform a hundred forms of penance and self-injury, and the result will be the same: The stain remains, and death terrifies. We know that our conscience is defiled—not with external things like touching a corpse or eating a piece of pork. Jesus said it is what comes out of a person that defiles, not what goes in (Mark 7:15-23). We are defiled by pride and self-pity and bitterness and lust and envy and jealousy and covetousness and apathy and fear—and the actions they breed. These are all "dead works." They have no spiritual life in them. They don't come from new life; they come from death, and they lead to death. That is why they make us feel hopeless in our consciences.

The only answer in these modern times, as in all other times, is the blood of Christ. When our conscience rises up and condemns us, where will we turn? We turn to Christ. We turn to the suffering and death of Christ—the blood of Christ. This is the only cleansing agent in the universe that can give the conscience relief in life and peace in death.

TO OBTAIN FOR US ALL THINGS THAT ARE GOOD FOR US

He who did not spare his own Son but gave him up for us all,
how will he not also with him graciously give us all things?

Romans 8:32

I love the logic of this verse. Not because I love logic, but because I love having my real needs met. The two halves of Romans 8:32 have a stupendously important logical connection. We may not see it, since the second half is a question: "How will he not also with him give us all things?" But if we change the question into the statement that it implies, we will see it. "He who did not spare his own Son but gave him up for us all, *will therefore surely* also with him graciously give us all things."

In other words, the connection between the two halves is meant to make the second half absolutely certain. If God did the hardest thing of all—namely, give up his own Son to suffering and death—then it is certain that he will do the comparatively easy thing, namely, give us all things with him. God's total commitment to give us all things is more sure than the sacrifice of his Son. He gave his Son "for us all." That done, could he stop being for us? It would be unthinkable.

But what does "give us all things" mean? Not an easy life of comfort. Not even safety from our enemies. We know this from what the Bible says four verses later: "For your sake we are being killed all the day long; we are regarded as sheep to be slaughtered" (Romans 8:36). Many Christians, even today, suffer this kind of persecution. When the Bible asks, "Shall tribulation, or distress, or persecution, or famine, or nakedness, or danger, or sword" separate us from the love of Christ (Romans 8:35), the answer is no. Not because these things don't happen to Christians, but because "in all these things we are more than conquerors through him who loved us" (Romans 8:37).

What then does it mean that because of Christ's death for us God will certainly with him graciously give us "all things"? It means that he will give us all things that are good for us. All things that we really need in order to be conformed to the image of his Son (Romans 8:29). All things we need in order to attain everlasting joy.

It's the same as the other biblical promise: "My God will supply *every need* of yours according to his riches in glory in Christ Jesus" (Philippians 4:19). This promise is clarified in the preceding words: "In any and every circumstance, I have learned the secret of facing plenty and *hunger*, abundance and *need*. I can do *all things* through him who strengthens me" (Philippians 4:12-13).

It says we can do "all things" through Christ. But notice "all things" includes "hungering" and "needing." God will meet every real need, including the ability to rejoice in suffering when many felt needs do not get met. God will meet every real need, including the need for grace to hunger when the felt need for food is not met. The suffering and death of Christ guarantee that God will give us all things that we need to do his will and to give him glory and to attain everlasting joy.

TO HEAL US FROM MORAL AND PHYSICAL SICKNESS

Upon him was the chastisement that brought us peace,
and with his stripes we are healed.

Isaiah 53:5

[He] healed all who were sick.
This was to fulfill what was spoken by the prophet Isaiah:
"He took our illnesses and bore our diseases."

Matthew 8:16-17

Christ suffered and died so that disease would one day be utterly destroyed. Disease and death were not part of God's original way with the world. They came in with sin as part of God's judgment on creation. The Bible says, "The creation was subjected to futility, not willingly, but because of him who subjected it, in hope" (Romans 8:20). God subjected the world to the futility of physical pain to show the horror of moral evil.

This futility included death. "Sin came into the world through one man, and death through sin" (Romans 5:12). It included all the groaning of disease. And Christians are not excluded: "Not only the creation, but we ourselves, who have the firstfruits of the Spirit [that is, those who trust Christ], groan inwardly as we wait eagerly for adoption as sons, the redemption of our bodies" (Romans 8:23).

But all this misery of disease is temporary. We look forward to a time when bodily pain will be no more. The subjection of creation to futility was not permanent. From the very beginning of his judgment, the Bible says God aimed at hope. His final purpose was this: "that the creation itself will be set free from its bondage to decay and obtain the freedom of the glory of the children of God" (Romans 8:21).

When Christ came into the world, he was on a mission to accomplish this global redemption. He signaled his purposes by healing many people during his lifetime. There were occasions when the crowds gathered and he "healed all who were sick" (Matthew 8:16; Luke 6:19). This was a preview of what was coming at the end of history when "he will wipe away every tear from their eyes, and death shall be no more, neither shall there be mourning nor crying nor pain anymore" (Revelation 21:4).

The way Christ defeated death and disease was by taking them on himself and carrying them with him to the grave. God's judgment on the sin that brought disease was endured by Jesus when he suffered and died. The prophet Isaiah explained the death of Christ with these words: "He was wounded for our transgressions; he was crushed for our iniquities; upon him was the chastisement that brought us peace, and *with his stripes we are healed*" (Isaiah 53:5). The horrible blows to the back of Jesus bought a world without disease.

One day all disease will be banished from God's redeemed creation. There will be a new earth. We will have new bodies. Death will be swallowed up by everlasting life (1 Corinthians 15:54; 2 Corinthians 5:4). "The wolf and the lamb shall graze together; the lion shall eat straw like the ox" (Isaiah 65:25). And all who love Christ will sing songs of thanks to the Lamb who was slain to redeem us from sin and death and disease.

TO GIVE ETERNAL LIFE TO ALL WHO BELIEVE ON HIM

*For God so loved the world, that he gave his only Son,
that whoever believes in him should not perish but have eternal life.*

John 3:16

In our happiest times we do not want to die. The wish for death rises only when our suffering seems unbearable. What we really want in those times is not death, but relief. We would love for the good times to come again. We would like the pain to go away. We would like to have our loved one back from the grave. We want life and happiness.

We are kidding ourselves when we romanticize death as the climax of a life well lived. It is an enemy. It cuts us off from all the wonderful pleasures of this world. We call death sweet names only as the lesser of evils. The executioner that delivers the *coup de grace* in our suffering is not the fulfillment of longing, but the end of hope. The longing of the human heart is to live and to be happy.

God made us that way. "He has put eternity into man's heart" (Ecclesiastes 3:11). We are created in God's image, and God loves life and lives forever. We were made to live forever. And we will. The opposite of eternal life is not annihilation. It is hell. Jesus spoke of it more than anybody, and he made plain that rejecting the eternal life he offered would result not in obliteration, but in the misery of God's wrath: "Whoever believes in the Son has eternal life; whoever does not obey the Son shall not see life, but the wrath of God remains on him" (John 3:36).

And it remains forever. Jesus said, "These will go away into eternal punishment, but the righteous into eternal life" (Matthew 25:46). This is an unspeakable reality that shows the infinite evil of treating God with indifference or contempt. So Jesus warns, "If your eye causes you to sin, tear it out. It is better for you to enter the kingdom of God with one eye than with two eyes to be thrown into hell, 'where their worm does not die and the fire is not quenched'" (Mark 9:47-48).

So eternal life is not merely the extension of this life with its mix of pain and pleasure. As hell is the worst outcome of this life, so "eternal life" is the best. It is supreme and ever-increasing happiness where all sin and all sadness will be gone. All that is evil and harmful in this fallen creation will be removed. All that is good—all that will bring true and lasting happiness—will be preserved and purified and intensified.

We will be changed so that we are capable of dimensions of happiness that were inconceivable to us in this life. "What no eye has seen, nor ear heard, nor the heart of man imagined . . . God has prepared for those who love him" (1 Corinthians 2:9). It is true every moment of life, now and always: For those who trust Christ the best is yet to come. We will see the all-satisfying glory of God. "This is eternal life, that they know you the only true God, and Jesus Christ whom you have sent" (John 17:3). For this Christ suffered and died. Why would we not embrace him as our treasure, and live?

To Deliver Us from the Present Evil Age

[He] gave himself for our sins to deliver us from the present evil age,
according to the will of our God and Father.

Galatians 1:4

Until we die, or until Christ returns to establish his kingdom, we live in "the present evil age." Therefore, when the Bible says that Christ gave himself "to deliver us from the present evil age," it does not mean that he will take us out of the world, but that he will deliver us from the power of the evil in it. Jesus prayed for us like this: "I do not ask that you take them out of the world, but that you keep them from the evil one" (John 17:15).

The reason Jesus prays for deliverance from "the evil one" is that "this present evil age" is the age when Satan is given freedom to deceive and destroy. The Bible says, "The whole world lies in the power of the evil one" (1 John 5:19). This "evil one" is called "the god of this world," and his main aim is to blind people to truth. "The god of this world has blinded the minds of the unbelievers, to keep them from seeing the light of the gospel of the glory of Christ" (2 Corinthians 4:4).

Until we waken to our darkened spiritual condition, we live in sync with "the present evil age" and the ruler of it. "You once walked, following the course of this world, following the prince of the power of the air, the spirit that is now at work in the sons of disobedience" (Ephesians 2:2). Without knowing it, we were lackeys of the devil. What felt like freedom was bondage. The Bible speaks straight to twenty-first-century fads, fun, and addictions when it says, "They promise them freedom, but they themselves are slaves of corruption. For whatever overcomes a person, to that he is enslaved" (2 Peter 2:19).

The resounding cry of freedom in the Bible is, "Do not be conformed to this world, but be transformed by the renewal of your mind" (Romans 12:2). In other words, be free! Don't be duped by the gurus of the age. They are here today and gone tomorrow. One enslaving fad follows another. Thirty years from now today's tattoos will not be marks of freedom, but indelible reminders of conformity.

The wisdom of this age is folly in view of eternity. "Let no one deceive himself. If anyone among you thinks that he is wise in this age, let him become a fool that he may become wise. For the wisdom of this world is folly with God" (1 Corinthians 3:18-19). "The word of the cross is folly to those who are perishing" (1 Corinthians 1:18). What then is the wisdom of God in this age? It is the great liberating death of Jesus Christ. The early followers of Jesus said, "We preach Christ crucified . . . the power of God and the wisdom of God" (1 Corinthians 1:23-24).

When Christ went to the cross, he set millions of captives free. He unmasked the devil's fraud and broke his power. That's what he meant on the eve of his crucifixion when he said, "Now will the ruler of this world be cast out" (John 12:31). Don't follow a defeated foe. Follow Christ. It is costly. You will be an exile in this age. But you will be free.

To Reconcile Us to God

For if while we were enemies we were reconciled to God
by the death of his Son, much more, now that
we are reconciled, shall we be saved by his life.

Romans 5:10

The reconciliation that needs to happen between sinful man and God goes both ways. Our attitude toward God must be changed from defiance to faith. And God's attitude to us must be changed from wrath to mercy. But the two are not the same. I need God's help to change; but God does not need mine. My change will have to come from outside of me, but God's change originates in his own nature. Which means that overall, it is not a change in God at all. It is God's own planned action to stop being against me and start being for me.

The all-important words are "while we were enemies." This is when "we were reconciled to God by the death of his Son" (Romans 5:10). While we were *enemies*. In other words, the first "change" was God's, not ours. We were still enemies. Not that we were consciously on the warpath. Most people don't feel conscious hostility to God. The hostility is manifest more subtly with a quiet insubordination and indifference. The Bible describes it like this: "The mind that is set on the flesh is hostile to God, for it does not submit to God's law; indeed, it cannot" (Romans 8:7).

While we were still like that, God put Christ forward to bear our wrath-kindling sins and make it possible for him to treat us with mercy alone. God's first act in reconciling us to himself was to remove the obstacle that made him irreconcilable, namely, the God-belittling guilt of our sin. "In Christ God was reconciling the world to himself, not counting their trespasses against them" (2 Corinthians 5:19).

When the ambassadors of Christ take this message to the world, they say, "We implore you on behalf of Christ, be reconciled to God" (2 Corinthians 5:20). Do they only mean: Change your attitude to God? No, they also mean: Receive the prior work of God in Christ to reconcile himself to you.

Consider this analogy of reconciliation among men. Jesus said, "If you are offering your gift at the altar and there remember that your brother has something against you, leave your gift there before the altar and go. First be reconciled to your brother, and then come and offer your gift" (Matthew 5:23-24). When he says, "Be reconciled to your brother," notice that it is the brother who must remove his judgment. The brother is the one who "has something against you," just as God has something against us. "Be reconciled to your brother" means do what you must so that your brother's judgment against you will be removed.

But when we hear the gospel of Christ, we find that God has already done that: He took the steps we could not take to remove his own judgment. He sent Christ to suffer in our place. The decisive reconciliation happened "while we were enemies." Reconciliation from our side is simply to receive what God has already done, the way we receive an infinitely valuable gift.

TO BRING US TO GOD

*Christ also suffered once for sins, the righteous
for the unrighteous, that he might bring us to God.*

1 Peter 3:18

*But now in Christ Jesus you who once were far off
have been brought near by the blood of Christ.*

Ephesians 2:13

When all is said and done, God is the gospel. Gospel means "good news." Christianity is not first theology, but news. It is like prisoners of war hearing by hidden radio that the allies have landed and rescue is only a matter of time. The guards wonder why all the rejoicing.

But what is the ultimate good in the good news? It all ends in one thing: God himself. All the words of the gospel lead to him, or they are not gospel. For example, salvation is not good news if it only saves from hell and not for God. Forgiveness is not good news if it only gives relief from guilt and doesn't open the way to God. Justification is not good news if it only makes us legally acceptable to God but doesn't bring fellowship with God. Redemption is not good news if it only liberates us from bondage but doesn't bring us to God. Adoption is not good news if it only puts us in the Father's family but not in his arms.

This is crucial. Many people seem to embrace the good news without embracing God. There is no sure evidence that we have a new heart just because we want to escape hell. That's a perfectly natural desire, not a supernatural one. It doesn't take a new heart to want the psychological relief of forgiveness, or the removal of God's wrath, or the inheritance of God's world. All these things are understandable without any spiritual change. You don't need to be born again to want these things. The devils want them.

It is not wrong to want them. Indeed it is folly not to. But the evidence that we have been changed is that we want these things because they bring us to the enjoyment of God. This is the greatest thing Christ died for. "Christ also suffered once for sins, the righteous for the unrighteous, *that he might bring us to God*" (1 Peter 3:18).

Why is this the essence of the good news? Because we were made to experience full and lasting happiness from seeing and savoring the glory of God. If our best joy comes from something less, we are idolaters and God is dishonored. He created us in such a way that his glory is displayed through our joy in it. The gospel of Christ is the good news that at the cost of his Son's life, God has done everything necessary to enthrall us with what will make us eternally and ever-increasingly happy, namely, himself.

Long before Christ came, God revealed himself as the source of full and lasting pleasure. "You make known to me the path of life; in your presence there is fullness of joy; at your right hand are pleasures forevermore" (Psalm 16:11). Then he sent Christ to suffer "that he might bring us to God." This means he sent Christ to bring us to the deepest, longest joy a human can have. Hear then the invitation: Turn from "the fleeting pleasures of sin" (Hebrews 11:25) and come to "pleasures forevermore." Come to Christ.

So That We Might Belong to Him

You also have died to the law through the body of Christ,
so that you may belong to another,
to him who has been raised from the dead.

Romans 7:4

You are not your own,
for you were bought with a price.

1 Corinthians 6:19-20

Care for the church of God,
which he obtained with his own blood.

Acts 20:28

The ultimate question is not *who* you are but *whose* you are. Of course, many people think they are nobody's slave. They dream of total independence. Like a jellyfish carried by the tides feels free because it isn't fastened down with the bondage of barnacles.

But Jesus had a word for people who thought that way. He said, "You will know the truth, and the truth will set you free." But they responded, "We . . . have never been enslaved to anyone. How is it that you say, 'You will become free'?" So Jesus answered, "Truly, truly, I say to you, everyone who commits sin is a slave to sin" (John 8:32-34).

The Bible gives no reality to fallen humans who are ultimately self-determining. There is no autonomy in the fallen world. We are governed by sin or governed by God. "You are slaves of the one whom you obey. . . . When you were slaves of sin, you were free in regard to righteousness. . . . But now . . . you have been set free from sin and have become slaves of God" (Romans 6:16, 20, 22).

Most of the time we are free to do what we want. But we are not free to want what we ought. For that we need a new power based on a divine purchase. The *power* is God's. Which is why the Bible says, "Thanks be to *God*, that you who were once slaves of sin have become obedient from the heart" (Romans 6:17). God is the one who may "grant them repentance leading to a knowledge of the truth, and they may escape from the snare of the devil, after being captured by him to do his will" (2 Timothy 2:25-26).

And the *purchase* that unleashes this power is the death of Christ. "You are not your own, for you were bought with a price" (1 Corinthians 6:19-20). And what price did Christ pay for those who trust him? "He obtained [them] with his own blood" (Acts 20:28).

Now we are free indeed. Not to be autonomous, but to want what is good. A whole new way of life opens to us when the death of Christ becomes the death of our old self. Relationship with the living Christ replaces rules. And the freedom of fruit-bearing replaces the bondage of law. "You also have died to the law through the body of Christ, *so that you may belong to another*, to him who has been raised from the dead, in order that we may bear fruit for God" (Romans 7:4).

Christ suffered and died that we might be set free from law and sin and belong to him. Here is where obedience ceases to be a burden and becomes the freedom of fruit-bearing. Remember, you are not your own. Whose will you be? If Christ's, then come and belong.

To Give Us Confident
Access to the Holiest Place

*We have confidence to enter the holy places
by the blood of Jesus.*
Hebrews 10:19

One of the great mysteries in the Old Testament was the meaning of the worship tent used by Israel called the "tabernacle." The mystery was hinted at but not clear. When the people of Israel came out of Egypt and arrived at Mount Sinai, God gave detailed instructions to Moses about how to build this mobile tent of worship with all its parts and furnishings. The mysterious thing about it was this command: "See that you make them after the pattern for them, which is being shown you on the mountain" (Exodus 25:40).

When Christ came into the world 1,400 years later, it was more fully revealed that this "pattern" for the old tabernacle was a "copy" or a "shadow" of realities in heaven. The tabernacle was an earthly figure of a heavenly reality. So in the New Testament we read this: "[The priests] serve a copy and shadow of the heavenly things. For when Moses was about to erect the tent, he was instructed by God, saying, 'See that you make everything according to the pattern that was shown you on the mountain'" (Hebrews 8:5).

So all the worship practices of Israel in the Old Testament point toward something more real. Just as there were holy rooms in the tabernacle, where the priest repeatedly took the blood of the animal sacrifices and met with God, so there are infinitely superior "holy places," as it were, in heaven, where Christ entered with his own blood, not repeatedly, but once for all.

> When Christ appeared as a high priest . . . through the greater and more perfect tent (not made with hands, that is, not of this creation) he entered once for all into the holy places, not by means of the blood of goats and calves but by means of his own blood, thus securing an eternal redemption. (Hebrews 9:11-12)

The implication of this for us is that the way is now opened for us to go with Christ into all the holiest places of God's presence. Formerly only the Jewish priests could go into the "copy" and "shadow" of these places. Only the high priest could go once a year into the most holy place where the glory of God appeared (Hebrews 9:7). There was a forbidding curtain protecting the place of glory. The Bible tells us that when Christ breathed his last on the cross, "the curtain of the temple was torn in two, from top to bottom. And the earth shook, and the rocks were split" (Matthew 27:51).

What did that mean? The interpretation is given in these words: "We have confidence to enter the holy places by the blood of Jesus, by the new and living way that he opened for us through the curtain, that is, through his flesh" (Hebrews 10:19-20). Without Christ the holiness of God had to be protected from us. He would have been dishonored, and we would have been consumed because of our sin. But now, because of Christ, we may come near and feast our hearts on the fullness of the flaming beauty of God's holiness. He will not be dishonored . We will not be consumed. Because of the all-protecting Christ, God will be honored, and we will stand in everlasting awe. Therefore, do not fear to come. But come through Christ.

TO BECOME FOR US THE PLACE WHERE WE MEET GOD

*Jesus answered them, "Destroy this temple, and in three days
I will raise it up." The Jews then said,
"It has taken forty-six years to build this temple,
and will you raise it up in three days?"
But he was speaking about the temple of his body.*

John 2:19-21

Kill me, and I will become the global meeting place with God."
That's the way I would paraphrase John 2:19-21. They
thought Jesus was referring to the temple in Jerusalem: "Destroy
this temple, and in three days I will raise it up." But he was referring to his body.

Why did Jesus draw the connection between the Jewish temple and his own body? Because he came to take the place of the
temple as the meeting place with God. With the coming of the Son
of God in human flesh, ritual and worship would undergo profound change. Christ himself would become the final Passover
lamb, the final priest, the final temple. They would all pass away,
and he would remain.

What remained would be infinitely better. Referring to himself,
Jesus said, "I tell you, something greater than the temple is here"
(Matthew 12:6). The temple became the dwelling of God at rare
times when the glory of God filled the holy place. But of Christ

the Bible says, "In him the whole fullness of deity dwells bodily" (Colossians 2:9). The presence of God does not come and go on Jesus. He is God. Where we meet him, we meet God.

God met the people in the temple through many imperfect human mediators. But now it is said of Christ, "There is one mediator between God and men, the man Christ Jesus" (1 Timothy 2:5). If we would meet God in worship, there is only one place we must go, to Jesus Christ. Christianity has no geographical center like Islam and Judaism.

Once when Jesus confronted a woman with her adultery, she changed the subject and said, "Our fathers worshiped on this mountain, but you say that in Jerusalem is the place where people ought to worship." Jesus followed her on the detour: "Woman, . . . the hour is coming when neither on this mountain nor in Jerusalem will you worship the Father." Geography is not the issue. What is? Jesus continued, "The hour is coming, and is now here, when the true worshipers will worship the Father in spirit and truth" (John 4:20-23).

Jesus changes the categories entirely. Not in this *mountain* or in that *city*, but in *spirit* and in *truth*. He came into the world to explode geographical limitation. There is no temple now. Jerusalem is not the center. Christ is. Do we want to see God? Jesus says, "Whoever has seen me has seen the Father" (John 14:9). Do we want to receive God? Jesus says, "Whoever receives me receives him who sent me" (Matthew 10:40). Do we want to have the presence of God in worship? The Bible says, "Whoever confesses the Son has the Father also" (1 John 2:23). Do we want to honor the Father? Jesus says, "Whoever does not honor the Son does not honor the Father who sent him" (John 5:23).

When Christ died and rose again, the old temple was replaced by the globally accessible Christ. You may come to him without moving a muscle. He is as close as faith.

To Bring the Old Testament Priesthood to an End and Become the Eternal High Priest

The former priests . . . were prevented by death from continuing in office, but he holds his priesthood permanently, because he continues forever. Consequently, he is able to save to the uttermost those who draw near to God through him, since he always lives to make intercession for them. . . . He has no need, like those high priests, to offer sacrifices daily, first for his own sins and then for those of the people, since he did this once for all when he offered up himself.

Hebrews 7:23-27

For Christ has entered . . . into heaven itself, now to appear in the presence of God on our behalf. Nor was it to offer himself repeatedly, as the high priest enters the holy places every year with blood not his own, for then he would have had to suffer repeatedly since the foundation of the world. But as it is, he has appeared once for all at the end of the ages to put away sin by the sacrifice of himself.

Hebrews 9:24-26

Every priest stands daily at his service, offering repeatedly the same sacrifices, which can never take away sins. But when Christ had offered for all time a single sacrifice for sins, he sat down at the right hand of God.

Hebrews 10:11-12

One of the greatest phrases of Christian truth is "once for all." It comes from one Greek word (*ephapax*) and means "once for all time." It means that something happened that was decisive. The act accomplished so much that it need never be repeated. Any effort to repeat it would discredit the achievement that happened "once for all."

It was a gloomy reality year after year that the priests in Israel had to offer animal sacrifices for their own sins and the sins of the people. I don't mean there was no forgiveness. God appointed these sacrifices for the relief of his people. They sinned and needed a substitute to bear their punishment. It was mercy that God accepted the ministry of sinful priests and substitute animals.

But there was a dark side to it. It had to be done over and over. The Bible says, "In these sacrifices there is a reminder of sin every year" (Hebrews 10:3). The people knew that when they laid their hands on the head of a bull to transfer their sins to the animal, it would all have to be done again. No animal could suffice to suffer for human sins. Sinful priests had to sacrifice for their own sins. Mortal priests had to be replaced. Bulls and goats had no moral life and could not bear the guilt of man. "It is impossible for the blood of bulls and goats to take away sins" (Hebrews 10:4).

But there was a silver lining around this cloud of priestly insufficiency. If God honored these inadequate things, it must mean that one day he would send a servant qualified to complete what these priests could not perform—to put away sin once for all.

That's who Jesus Christ is. He became the final Priest and the final Sacrifice. *Sinless*, he did not offer sacrifices for himself. *Immortal*, he never has to be replaced. *Human*, he could bear human sins. Therefore he did not offer sacrifices for himself; he offered himself as the final sacrifice. There will never be the need for another. There is one mediator between us and God. One priest. We need no other. Oh, how happy are those who draw near to God through Christ alone.

TO BECOME A SYMPATHETIC AND HELPFUL PRIEST

For we do not have a high priest who is unable to sympathize with our weaknesses, but one who in every respect has been tempted as we are, yet without sin. Let us then with confidence draw near to the throne of grace, that we may receive mercy and find grace to help in time of need.

Hebrews 4:15-16

Christ became our Priest by the sacrifice of himself on the cross (Hebrews 9:26). He is our go-between with God. His obedience and suffering were so perfect that God will not turn him away. Therefore, if we go to God through him, God will not turn us away either.

But it gets even better. On the way to the cross for thirty years, Christ was tempted like every human is tempted. True, he never sinned. But wise people have pointed out that this means his temptations were stronger than ours, not weaker. If a person gives in to temptation, it never reaches its fullest and longest assault. We capitulate while the pressure is still building. But Jesus never did. So he endured the full pressure to the end and never caved. He knows what it is to be tempted with fullest force.

A lifetime of temptation climaxing in spectacular abuse and abandonment gave Jesus an unparalleled ability to sympathize with tempted and suffering people. No one has ever suffered more.

No one has ever endured more abuse. And no one ever deserved it less or had a greater right to fight back. But the apostle Peter said, "He committed no sin, neither was deceit found in his mouth. When he was reviled, he did not revile in return; when he suffered, he did not threaten, but continued entrusting himself to him who judges justly" (1 Peter 2:22-23).

Therefore, the Bible says he is able "to sympathize with our weaknesses" (Hebrews 4:15). This is amazing. The risen Son of God in heaven at God's right hand with all authority over the universe feels what we feel when we come to him in sorrow or pain—or cornered with the promises of sinful pleasure.

What difference does this make? The Bible answers by making a connection between Jesus' sympathy and our confidence in prayer. It says that since he is able to "sympathize with our weaknesses . . . [*therefore* we should] with confidence draw near to the throne of grace, that we may receive mercy and find grace to help in time of need" (Hebrews 4:15-16).

Evidently the thought goes like this: We are likely to feel unwelcome in the presence of God if we come with struggles. We feel God's purity and perfection so keenly that everything about us seems unsuitable in his presence. But then we remember that Jesus is "sympathetic." He feels *with* us, not *against* us. This awareness of Christ's sympathy makes us bold to come. He knows our cry. He tasted our struggle. He bids us come with confidence when we feel our need. So let's remember the old song of John Newton:

> *Thou art coming to a King.*
> *Large petitions with thee bring;*
> *For his grace and pow'r are such*
> *None can ever ask too much.*[4]

TO FREE US FROM THE FUTILITY OF OUR ANCESTRY

*You were ransomed from the futile ways inherited from
your forefathers, not with perishable things such as silver or gold,
but with the precious blood of Christ,
like that of a lamb without blemish or spot.*

1 Peter 1:18-19

Secular people in the West, and more primitive people in animistic tribes, have this in common: They believe in the power of ancestral bondage. They call it by different names. Animistic people may speak in terms of ancestral spirits and the transmission of curses. Secular people may speak of genetic influence or the wounding of abusive, codependent, emotionally distant parents. In both cases there is a sense of fatalism that we are bound to live with the curse or the wounds from our ancestry. The future seems futile and void of happiness.

When the Bible says, "You were ransomed from the futile ways inherited from your forefathers," it is referring to an empty, meaningless, unprofitable way of living that ends with destruction. It says that these "futile ways" are connected with our ancestors. It doesn't say how. The crucial thing is to notice how we are freed from the bondage of this futility. The power of the liberator defines the extent of the liberation.

The liberation from ancestral bondage happens "not with perishable things such as silver or gold." Silver and gold represent the most valuable things that could be paid for our ransom. But we all know they are useless. The richest people are often the most enslaved to the futility. A wealthy tribal chief may be tormented by the fear of an ancestral hex on his life. A secular president of a successful company may be driven by unconscious forces from his background that ruin his marriage and children.

Silver and gold are powerless to help. The suffering and death of Jesus provide what is needed: not gold or silver but "the precious blood of Christ, like that of a lamb without blemish or spot." When Christ died, God had a view to the relationship between us and our ancestors. He meant to set us free from the futility we inherited from them. That is one of the great reasons Christ died.

No hex can hold against you, if your sins are all forgiven, and you are clothed with the righteousness of Christ, and you are ransomed and loved by the Creator of the universe. The suffering and death of Jesus is the final reason why the Bible says of God's people, "There is no enchantment against Jacob, no divination against Israel" (Numbers 23:23). When Jesus died, all the blessings of heaven were purchased for those who trust him. And when God blesses, none can curse.

Nor is any wound that was inflicted by a parent beyond the healing of Jesus. The healing ransom is called "the precious blood of Christ." The word "precious" conveys infinite value. Therefore the ransom is infinitely liberating. No bondage can stand against it. Therefore, let us turn from silver and gold and embrace the gift of God.

To Free Us from the Slavery of Sin

*To him who loves us and has freed us from our sins by his blood
and made us a kingdom, priests to his God and Father,
to him be glory and dominion forever and ever.*

Revelation 1:5-6

*Jesus also suffered outside the gate
in order to sanctify the people through his own blood.*

Hebrews 13:12

Our sin ruins us in two ways. It makes us guilty before God, so that we are under his just condemnation; and it makes us ugly in our behavior, so that we disfigure the image of God we were meant to display. It damns us with guilt, and it enslaves us to lovelessness.

The blood of Jesus frees us from both miseries. It satisfies God's righteousness so that our sins can be justly forgiven. And it defeats the power of sin to make us slaves to lovelessness. We have seen how Christ absorbs the wrath of God and takes away our guilt. But now how does the blood of Christ liberate us from the slavery of sin?

The answer is not that he is a powerful example to us and inspires us to free ourselves from selfishness. Oh, yes, Jesus is an example to us. And a very powerful one. He clearly meant for us to imitate him: "A new commandment I give to you, that you love one another: just as I have loved you, you also are to love one another" (John 13:34). But the call to imitation is not the power of liberation. There is something deeper.

Sin is such a powerful influence in our lives that we must be liberated by God's power, not by our willpower. But since we are sinners we must ask, Is the power of God directed toward our liberation or our condemnation? That's where the suffering of Christ comes in. When Christ died to remove our condemnation, he opened, as it were, the valve of heaven's mighty mercy to flow on behalf of our liberation from the power of sin.

In other words, rescue from the *guilt* of sin and the wrath of God had to precede rescue from the *power* of sin by the mercy of God. The crucial biblical words for saying this are: *Justification* precedes and secures *sanctification*. They are different. One is an instantaneous declaration (not guilty!); the other is an ongoing transformation.

Now, for those who are trusting Christ, the power of God is not in the service of his condemning wrath, but his liberating mercy. God gives us this power for change through the person of his Holy Spirit. That is why the beauty of "love, joy, peace, patience, kindness, goodness, faithfulness, gentleness, self-control" are called "the fruit of the Spirit" (Galatians 5:22-23). This is why the Bible can make the amazing promise: "Sin will have no dominion over you, since you are not under law but under grace" (Romans 6:14). Being "under grace" secures the omnipotent power of God to destroy our lovelessness (not all at once, but progressively). We are not passive in the defeat of our selfishness, but neither do we provide the decisive power. It is God's grace. Hence the great apostle Paul said, "I worked harder than any of them, though it was not I, but the grace of God that is with me" (1 Corinthians 15:10). May the God of all grace, by faith in Christ, free us from both the guilt and slavery of sin.

THAT WE MIGHT DIE TO SIN AND LIVE TO RIGHTEOUSNESS

He himself bore our sins in his body on the tree,
that we might die to sin and live to righteousness.

1 Peter 2:24

Strange as it may sound, Christ's dying in our place and for our sins means that *we* died. You would think that having a substitute die in your place would mean that you escape death. And, of course, we do escape death—the *eternal* death of endless misery and separation from God. Jesus said, "I give them eternal life, and they will *never perish*" (John 10:28). "Everyone who lives and believes in me *shall never die*" (John 11:26). The death of Jesus *does* indeed mean that "whoever believes in him should *not perish* but have eternal life" (John 3:16).

But there is another sense in which we die precisely because Christ died in our place and for our sins. "He himself bore our sins in his body on the tree, that we might die . . ." (1 Peter 2:24). He died that we might live; and he died that we might die. When Christ died, I, as a believer in Christ, died with him. The Bible is clear: "We have been united with him in a death like his" (Romans 6:5). "One has died for all, therefore all have died" (2 Corinthians 5:14).

Faith is the evidence of being united to Christ in this profound way. Believers "have been crucified with Christ" (Galatians 2:20).

We look back on his death and know that, in the mind of God, we were there. Our sins were on him, and the death we deserved was happening to us in him. Baptism signifies this death with Christ. "We were buried . . . with him *by baptism* into death" (Romans 6:4). The water is like a grave. Going under is a picture of death. Coming up is a picture of new life. And it is all a picture of what God is doing "through faith." "[You have] been buried with him in baptism, in which you were also raised with him *through faith* in the powerful working of God" (Colossians 2:12).

The fact that I died with Christ is linked directly to his dying for my sin. "He himself *bore our sins . . . that we might die.*" This means that when I embrace Jesus as my Savior, I embrace my own death as a sinner. My sin brought Jesus to the grave and brought me there with him. Faith sees sin as murderous. It killed Jesus, and it killed me.

Therefore, becoming a Christian means death to sin. The old self that loved sin died with Jesus. Sin is like a prostitute that no longer looks beautiful. She is the murderer of my King and myself. Therefore, the believer is dead to sin, no longer dominated by her attractions. Sin, the prostitute who killed my friend, has no appeal. She has become an enemy.

My new life is now swayed by righteousness. "He himself bore our sins in his body on the tree, that we might . . . *live to righteousness*" (1 Peter 2:24). The beauty of Christ, who loved me and gave himself for me, is the desire of my soul. And his beauty is perfect righteousness. The command that I now love to obey is this (and I invite you to join me): "Present yourselves to God as those who have been brought from death to life, and your members to God as instruments for righteousness" (Romans 6:13).

So That We Would Die to the Law and Bear Fruit for God

*You also have died to the law through the body of Christ,
so that you may belong to another, to him who has been raised
from the dead, in order that we may bear fruit for God.*

Romans 7:4

When Christ died for us, we died with him. God looked on us who believe as united to Christ. His death for our sin was our death in him. (See the previous chapter.) But sin was not the only reality that killed Jesus and us. So did the law of God. When we break the law by sinning, the law sentences us to death. If there were no law, there would be no punishment. "For . . . where there is no law there is no transgression" (Romans 4:15). But "whatever the law says it speaks to those who are under the law, so that . . . the whole world may be held accountable to God" (Romans 3:19).

There was no escape from the curse of he law. It was just; we were guilty. There was only one way to be free: Someone must pay the penalty. That's why Jesus came: "Christ redeemed us from the curse of the law by becoming a curse for us" (Galatians 3:13).

Therefore, God's law cannot condemn us if we are in Christ. Its power to rule us is doubly broken. On the one hand, the law's demands have been fulfilled by Christ on our behalf. His perfect law-keeping is credited to our account (see chapter 11). On the other hand, the law's penalty has been paid by the blood of Christ.

This is why the Bible so clearly teaches that getting right with God is not based on law-keeping. "By works of the law no human being will be justified in his sight" (Romans 3:20). "A person is not justified by works of the law but through faith in Jesus Christ" (Galatians 2:16). There is no hope of getting right with God by law-keeping. The only hope is the blood and righteousness of Christ, which is ours by faith alone. "We hold that one is justified by faith apart from works of the law" (Romans 3:28).

How then do we please God, if we are dead to his law and it is no longer our master? Is not the law the expression of God's good and holy will (Romans 7:12)? The biblical answer is that instead of belonging to the law, which demands and condemns, we now belong to Christ who demands and gives. Formerly, righteousness was demanded from outside in letters written in stone. But now righteousness rises within us as a longing in our relationship with Christ. He is present and real. By his Spirit he helps us in our weakness. A living person has replaced a lethal list. "The letter kills, but the Spirit gives life" (2 Corinthians 3:6). (See chapter 14.)

This is why the Bible says that the new way of obedience is *fruit-bearing*, not law-keeping. "You . . . have died to the law through the body of Christ, so that you may belong to another, to him who has been raised from the dead, *in order that we may bear fruit for God*" (Romans 7:4). We have died to law-keeping so that we might live to fruit-bearing. Fruit grows naturally on a tree. If the tree is good, the fruit will be good. And the tree, in this case, is a living relationship of love to Jesus Christ. For this he died. Now he bids us come: "Trust me." Die to the law, that you might bear the fruit of love.

TO ENABLE US TO LIVE FOR CHRIST AND NOT OURSELVES

*He died for all, that those who live might no longer live
for themselves but for him who for their sake died and was raised.*

2 Corinthians 5:15

It troubles a lot of people that Christ died to exalt Christ. Boiled down to its essence, 2 Corinthians 5:15 says Christ died for us that we might live for him. In other words, he died for us so that we make much of him. Bluntly, Christ died for Christ.

Now that is true. It's not a word trick. The very essence of sin is that we have failed to glorify God—which includes failing to glorify his Son (Romans 3:23). But Christ died to bear that sin and to free us from it. So he died to bear the dishonor that we had heaped on him by our sin. He died to turn this around. Christ died for the glory of Christ.

The reason this troubles people is that it sounds vain. It doesn't seem like a loving thing to do. So it seems to turn the suffering of Christ into the very opposite of what the Bible says it is, namely, the supreme act of love. But in fact it's both. Christ's dying for his own glory and his dying to show love are not only both *true*, they are both *the same*.

Christ is unique. No one else can act this way and call it love. Christ is the only human in the universe who is also God and therefore infinitely valuable. He is infinitely beautiful in all his moral perfections. He is infinitely wise and just and good and strong. "He is the radiance of the glory of God and the exact imprint of his nature" (Hebrews 1:3). To see him and know him is more satisfying than having all that earth can offer.

Those who knew him best spoke this way:

> *Whatever gain I had, I counted as loss for the sake of Christ. Indeed, I count everything as loss because of the surpassing worth of knowing Christ Jesus my Lord. For his sake I have suffered the loss of all things and count them as rubbish, in order that I may gain Christ. (Philippians 3:7-8)*

"Christ died that we might live for him" does not mean "that we might *help* him." "[God is not] served by human hands, as though he needed anything" (Acts 17:25). Neither is Christ: "The Son of Man came *not to be served* but to serve, and to give his life as a ransom for many" (Mark 10:45). What Christ died for is not that we might help him, but that we might see and savor him as infinitely valuable. He died to wean us from poisonous pleasures and enthrall us with the pleasures of his beauty. In this way we are loved, and he is honored. These are not competing aims. They are one.

Jesus said to his disciples that he had to go away so that he could send the Holy Spirit, the Helper (John 16:7). Then he told them what the Helper would do when he came: "He will glorify me" (John 16:14). Christ died and rose so that we would see and magnify him. This is the greatest help in the world. This is love. The most loving prayer Jesus ever prayed was this: "Father, I desire that they also, whom you have given me, may be with me where I am, to see my glory" (John 17:24). For this Christ died. This is love—suffering to give us everlasting enjoyment, namely himself.

TO MAKE HIS CROSS THE GROUND OF ALL OUR BOASTING

*Far be it from me to boast except in the cross of our
Lord Jesus Christ, by which the world has been crucified
to me, and I to the world.*

Galatians 6:14

This seems over the top. Boast only in the cross! Really? Literally *only* in the cross? Even the Bible talks about other things to boast in. Boast in the glory of God (Romans 5:2). Boast in our tribulations (Romans 5:3). Boast in our weaknesses (2 Corinthians 12:9). Boast in the people of Christ (1 Thessalonians 2:19). What does "only" mean here?

It means that all other boasting should still be a boasting in the cross. If we boast in the hope of glory, that very boast should be a boast in the cross of Christ. If we boast in the people of Christ, that very boasting should be a boasting in the cross. Boasting only in the cross means only the cross enables every other legitimate boast, and every legitimate boast should therefore honor the cross.

Why? Because every good thing—indeed, even every bad thing that God turns for good—was obtained for us by the cross of Christ. Apart from faith in Christ, sinners get only judgment. Yes, there are many pleasant things that come to unbelievers.

But the Bible teaches that even these natural blessings of life will only increase the severity of God's judgment in the end, if they are not received with thanks on the basis of Christ's sufferings (Romans 2:4-5).

Therefore, everything that we enjoy, as people who trust Christ, is owing to his death. His suffering absorbed all the judgment that guilty sinners deserved and purchased all the good that forgiven sinners enjoy. Therefore all our boasting in these things should be a boasting in the cross of Christ. We are not as Christ-centered and cross-cherishing as we should be, because we do not ponder the truth that everything good, and everything bad that God turns for the good, was purchased by the sufferings of Christ.

And how do we become that radically cross-focused? We must awaken to the truth that when Christ died on the cross, we died (see chapter 31). When this happened to the apostle Paul, he said, "The world has been crucified to me, and I to the world" (Galatians 6:14). This is the key to Christ-centered boasting in the cross.

When you put your trust in Christ, the overpowering attraction of the world is broken. You are a corpse to the world, and the world is a corpse to you. Or to put it positively, you are a "new creation" (Galatians 6:15). The old you is dead. A new you is alive—the you of faith in Christ. And what marks this faith is that it treasures Christ above everything in the world. The power of the world to woo your love away has died.

Being dead to the world means that every legitimate pleasure in the world becomes a blood-bought evidence of Christ's love and an occasion of boasting in the cross. When our hearts run back along the beam of blessing to the source in the cross, then the worldliness of the blessing is dead, and Christ crucified is everything.

TO ENABLE US TO LIVE BY FAITH IN HIM

*I have been crucified with Christ. It is no longer I who live,
but Christ who lives in me. And the life I now live in the flesh
I live by faith in the Son of God, who loved me
and gave himself for me.*

Galatians 2:20

There is an explicit paradox in this verse. "I have been crucified," but "I now live." But you might say, "That's not paradoxical, it's just sequential. First I died with Christ; then I was raised with him and now live." True. But what about these even more paradoxical words: "It is no longer I who live," yet "I now live"? Do I live or don't I?

Paradoxes are not contradictions. They just sound that way. What Paul means is that there was an "I" who died, and there is a different "I" who lives. That's what it means to become a Christian. An old self dies. A new self is "created" or "raised." "If anyone is in Christ, he is a new *creation*" (2 Corinthians 5:17). "When we were dead in our trespasses, [God] made us alive together with Christ . . . and *raised* us up with him" (Ephesians 2:5-6).

The aim of the death of Christ was to take our "old self" with him into the grave and put an end to it. "We know that our *old self* was crucified with him in order that the body of sin might be brought to nothing" (Romans 6:6). If we trust Christ, we are united to him, and God counts our old self as dying with Christ. The purpose was the raising of a new self.

So who is the new self? What's different about these two selves? Am I still me? The verse at the beginning of this chapter describes the new self in two ways: One way is almost unimaginable; the other is plain. First, it says that the new self is Christ living in me: "It is no longer I who live, but Christ who lives in me." I take this to mean that the new self is defined by Christ's presence and help at all times. He is always imparting life to me. He is always strengthening me for what he calls me to do. That's why the Bible says, "I can do all things through him who strengthens me" (Philippians 4:13). "I toil . . . with all his energy that he powerfully works within me" (Colossians 1:29). So when all is said and done the new self says, "I will not venture to speak of anything except what Christ has accomplished through me" (Romans 15:18).

That's the first way Galatians 2:20 speaks of the new self: a Christ-inhabited, Christ-sustained, Christ-strengthened me. That's what Christ died to bring about. That's what a Christian is. The other way it speaks of the new self is this: It lives by trusting Christ moment by moment. "The life I now live in the flesh I live by faith in the Son of God, who loved me and gave himself for me."

Without this second description of the new self, we might wonder what our part is in experiencing Christ's daily help. Now we have the answer: faith. From the divine side, Christ is living in us and enabling us to live the way he teaches us to live. It's his work. But from our side, it's experienced by trusting him moment by moment to be with us and to help us. The proof that he will be with us and will help us do this is the fact that he suffered and died to make it happen.

To Give Marriage Its Deepest Meaning

*Husbands, love your wives, as Christ loved the church
and gave himself up for her.*
Ephesians 5:25

God's design for marriage in the Bible pictures the husband loving his wife the way Christ loves his people, and the wife responding to her husband the way Christ's people should respond to him. This picture was in God's mind when he sent Christ into the world. Christ came for his bride and died for her to display the way marriage was meant to be.

No, the point of the analogy is not that husbands should suffer at the hands of their wives. It's true, that did happen to Jesus in a sense. He suffered in order to bring a people—a bride—into being, and these very people were among those who caused his suffering. And much of his sorrow was because his disciples abandoned him (Matthew 26:56). But the point of the analogy is how Jesus loved them to the point of death and did not cast them away.

God's idea for marriage preceded the union of Adam and Eve and the coming of Christ. We know this because when Christ's apostle explained the mystery of marriage, he reached back to the beginning of the Bible and quoted Genesis 2:24, "A man shall leave his father and mother and hold fast to his wife, and the two shall become one flesh." Then in the next sentence he interpreted what he had just quoted: "This mystery is profound, and I am saying that it refers to Christ and the church" (Ephesians 5:31-32).

That means that in God's mind marriage was designed in the beginning to display Christ's relationship to his people. The reason marriage is called a "mystery" is that this aim for marriage was not clearly revealed until the coming of Christ. Now we see that marriage is meant to make Christ's love for his people more visible in the world.

Since this was in God's mind from the beginning, it was also in Christ's mind when he faced death. He knew that among the many effects of his suffering was this: making the deepest meaning of marriage plain. All his sufferings were meant to be a message especially to husbands: This is how every husband should love his wife.

Even though God did not aim, in the beginning, for marriages to be miserable, many are. That's what sin does. It makes us treat each other badly. Christ suffered and died to change that. Wives have their responsibility in this change. But Christ gives a special responsibility to husbands. That's why the Bible says, "Husbands, love your wives, as Christ loved the church and gave himself up for her" (Ephesians 5:25).

Husbands are not Christ. But they are called to be like him. And the specific point of likeness is the husband's readiness to suffer for his wife's good without threatening or abusing her. This includes suffering to protect her from any outside forces that would harm her, as well as suffering disappointments or abuses even from her. This kind of love is possible because Christ died for both husband and wife. Their sins are forgiven. Neither needs to make the other suffer for sins. Christ has borne that suffering. Now as two sinful and forgiven people we can return good for evil.

TO CREATE A PEOPLE
PASSIONATE FOR GOOD WORKS

*[He] gave himself for us to redeem us from all lawlessness
and to purify for himself a people for his own possession
who are zealous for good works.*

Titus 2:14

At the heart of Christianity is the truth that we are forgiven and accepted by God, not because we have done good works, but to make us able and zealous to do them. The Bible says, "[God] saved us . . . not because of our works" (2 Timothy 1:9). Good deeds are not the *foundation* of our acceptance, but the *fruit* of it. Christ suffered and died not because we presented to him good works, but he died "to purify for himself a people . . . zealous for good works" (Titus 2:14).

This is the meaning of grace. We cannot obtain a right standing with God because of our works. It must be a free gift. We can only receive it by faith, cherishing it as our great treasure. This is why the Bible says, "By grace you have been saved through faith. And this is not your own doing; it is the gift of God, not a result of works, so that no one may boast" (Ephesians 2:8-9). Christ suffered and died so that good works would be the *effect*, not the cause, of our acceptance.

Not surprisingly, then, the next sentence says, "For we are . . . created in Christ Jesus for good works" (Ephesians 2:10). That is, we are saved *for* good works, not *by* good works. And the aim of Christ is not the mere *ability* to do them, but *passion* to do them. That's why the Bible uses the word "zealous." Christ died to make us "*zealous* for good works." Zeal means passion. Christ did not die to make good works merely possible or to produce a half-hearted pursuit. He died to produce in us a *passion* for good deeds. Christian purity is not the mere avoidance of evil, but the pursuit of good.

There are reasons why Jesus paid the infinite price to produce our passion for good deeds. He gave the main reason in these words: "Let your light shine before others, so that they may see your good works and give glory to your Father who is in heaven" (Matthew 5:16). God is shown to be glorious by the good deeds of Christians. For that glory Christ suffered and died.

When God's forgiveness and acceptance have freed us from fear and pride and greed, we are filled with a zeal to love others the way we have been loved. We risk our possessions and our lives since we are secure in Christ. When we love others like this, our behavior is contrary to human self-enhancement and self-preservation. Attention is thus drawn to our life-transforming Treasure and Security, namely, God.

And what are these "good works"? Without limiting their scope, the Bible means mainly helping people in urgent need, especially those who possess least and suffer most. For example, the Bible says, "Let our people learn to devote themselves to good works, so as to help cases of urgent need" (Titus 3:14). Christ died to make us this kind of people—passionate to help the poor and the perishing. It is the best life, no matter what it costs us in this world: They get help, we get joy, God gets glory.

TO CALL US TO FOLLOW HIS EXAMPLE OF LOWLINESS AND COSTLY LOVE

This is a gracious thing, when, mindful of God, one endures sorrows
while suffering unjustly. . . . For to this you have been called,
because Christ also suffered for you, leaving you an example,
so that you might follow in his steps.

1 Peter 2:19-21

Consider him who endured from sinners such hostility
against himself, so that you may not grow weary or fainthearted.
In your struggle against sin you have not yet resisted
to the point of shedding your blood.

Hebrews 12:3-4

Have this mind among yourselves, which is yours in Christ Jesus,
who, though he was in the form of God,
did not count equality with God a thing to be grasped,
but made himself nothing, taking the form of a servant,
being born in the likeness of men.
And being found in human form,
he humbled himself by becoming obedient
to the point of death, even death on a cross.

Philippians 2:5-8

Imitation is not salvation. But salvation brings imitation. Christ is not given to us first as model, but as Savior. In the experience of the believer, first comes the pardon of Christ, then the pattern of Christ. In the experience of Christ himself, they happen together: The same suffering that pardons our sins provides our pattern of love.

In fact, only when we experience the pardon of Christ can he become a pattern for us. This sounds wrong because his sufferings are unique. They cannot be imitated. No one but the Son of God can suffer "for us" the way Christ did. He bore our sins in a way that no one else could. He was a substitute sufferer. We can never duplicate this. It was once for all, the righteous for the unrighteous. Divine, vicarious suffering for sinners is inimitable.

However, this unique suffering, after pardoning and justifying sinners, transforms them into people who act like Jesus—not like him in pardoning, but like him in loving. Like him in suffering to do good to others. Like him in not returning evil for evil. Like him in lowliness and meekness. Like him in patient endurance. Like him in servanthood. Jesus suffered for us uniquely, that we might suffer with him in the cause of love.

Christ's apostle, Paul, said that his ambition was first to share in Christ's righteousness by faith, and then to share in his sufferings in ministry. "[May I] be found in [Christ], not having a righteousness of my own that comes from the law, but that which comes through faith in Christ . . . that I may . . . share his sufferings, becoming like him in his death" (Philippians 3:9-10). Justification precedes and makes possible imitation. Christ's suffering for justification makes possible our suffering for proclamation. Our suffering for others does not remove the wrath of God. It shows the value of having the wrath of God removed by the suffering of Christ. It points people to him.

When the Bible calls us to "endure everything for the sake of the elect, that they also may obtain the salvation that is in Christ Jesus" (2 Timothy 2:10), it means that our imitation of Christ points people to him who alone can save. Our suffering is crucial, but Christ's alone saves. Therefore, let us imitate his love, but not take his place.

To Create a Band of Crucified Followers

*If anyone would come after me,
let him deny himself and take up his cross daily
and follow me.*

Luke 9:23

*Whoever does not take his cross and follow me
is not worthy of me.*

Matthew 10:38

Christ died to create comrades on the Calvary road. Calvary is the name of the hill where he was crucified. He knew that the path of his life would take him there eventually. In fact, "he set his face" to go there (Luke 9:51). Nothing would hinder his mission to die. He knew where and when it had to happen. When someone warned him, on the way to Jerusalem, that he was in danger from King Herod, he scorned the idea that Herod could short-circuit God's plan. "Go and tell that fox, 'Behold, I cast out demons and perform cures today and tomorrow, and the third day I finish my course'" (Luke 13:32). All was proceeding according to plan. And when the end finally came and the mob arrested him the night before he died, he said to them, "All this has taken place that the Scriptures of the prophets might be fulfilled" (Matthew 26:56).

In a sense, the Calvary road is where everyone meets Jesus. It's true that he has already walked the road, and died, and risen, and now reigns in heaven until he comes again. But when Christ meets a person today, it is always on the Calvary road—on the way to the cross. Every time he meets someone on the Calvary road he says, "If anyone would come after me, let him deny himself and take up his cross daily and follow me" (Luke 9:23). When Christ went to the cross, his aim was to call a great band of believers after him.

The reason for this is not that Jesus must die again today, but that *we* must. When he bids us take up our cross, he means come and die. The cross was a place of horrible execution. It would have been unthinkable in Jesus' day to wear a cross as a piece of jewelry. It would have been like wearing a miniature electric chair or lynching rope. His words must have had a terrifying effect: "Whoever does not take his cross and follow me is not worthy of me" (Matthew 10:38).

So today the words are sobering. They mean at least that when I follow Jesus as my Savior and Lord, the old self-determining, self-absorbed me must be crucified. I must every day reckon myself dead to sin and alive to God. This is the path of life: "Consider yourselves dead to sin and alive to God in Christ Jesus" (Romans 6:11).

But camaraderie on the Calvary road means more. It means that Jesus died so that we would be willing to bear his reproach. "Jesus . . . suffered outside the gate. . . . Therefore let us go to him outside the camp and bear the reproach he endured" (Hebrews 13:12-13). But not just reproach. If necessary, martyrdom. The Bible pictures some of Christ's followers this way: "They have conquered [Satan] by the blood of the Lamb and by the word of their testimony, for they loved not their lives even unto death" (Revelation 12:11). So the Lamb of God shed his blood that we might defeat the devil by trusting his blood and shedding ours. Jesus calls us onto the Calvary road. It is a hard and good life. Come.

TO FREE US FROM BONDAGE TO THE FEAR OF DEATH

Since therefore the children share in flesh and blood,
he himself likewise partook of the same things,
that through death he might destroy the one who has the
power of death, that is, the devil, and deliver all those who
through fear of death were subject to lifelong slavery.

Hebrews 2:14-15

Jesus called Satan a murderer. "He was a murderer from the beginning, and has nothing to do with the truth . . . he is a liar and the father of lies" (John 8:44). But his main interest is not killing. It is damning. In fact, he much prefers that his followers have long and happy lives—to mock suffering saints and hide the horrors of hell.

His power to damn human beings lies not in himself, but in the sins that he inspires and the lies that he tells. The only thing that damns anybody is unforgiven sin. Hexes, enchantments, voodoo, séances, curses, black magic, apparitions, voices—none of these casts a person into hell. They are the bells and whistles of the devil. The one lethal weapon he has is the power to deceive us. His chief lie is that self-exaltation is more to be desired than Christ-exaltation, and sin preferable to righteousness. If that weapon could be taken out of his hand, he would no longer have the power of eternal death.

That is what Christ came to do—take that weapon out of Satan's hand. To do this, Christ took our sins on himself and suffered for them. When that happened, they could be used no more by the devil to destroy us. Taunt us? Yes. Mock us? Yes. But damn us? No. Christ bore the curse in our place. Try as he will, Satan cannot destroy us. The wrath of God is removed. His mercy is our shield. And Satan cannot succeed against us.

To accomplish this deliverance, Christ had to take on a human nature, because without it, he could not experience death. Only the death of the Son of God could destroy the one who had the power of death. Hence the Bible says, "Since . . . the children share in flesh and blood [=had a human nature], he himself likewise partook of the same things [=took on a human nature], that through death he might destroy the one who has the power of death, that is, the devil" (Hebrews 2:14). When Christ died for sins, he took from the devil his one lethal weapon: unforgiven sin.

Freedom from fear was the aim of Christ in doing this. By dying he delivered "all those who through fear of death were subject to lifelong slavery" (Hebrews 2:14). The fear of death enslaves. It makes us timid and dull. Jesus died to set us free. When the fear of death is destroyed by an act of self-sacrificing love, the bondage to boring, bigheaded self-preservation is broken. We are freed to love like Christ, even at the cost of our lives.

The devil may kill our body, but he can no longer kill our soul. It is safe in Christ. And even our mortal body will be raised someday: "He who raised Christ Jesus from the dead will also give life to your mortal bodies through his Spirit who dwells in you" (Romans 8:11). We are the freest of all people. And the Bible is unmistakable in what this freedom is for: "You were called to freedom, brothers. Only do not use your freedom as an opportunity for the flesh, but through love serve one another" (Galatians 5:13).

SO THAT WE WOULD BE WITH HIM IMMEDIATELY AFTER DEATH

*[He] died for us so that whether we are awake or asleep
we might live with him.*

1 Thessalonians 5:10

*To live is Christ, and to die is gain. . . .
I am hard pressed between the two. My desire is to depart
and be with Christ, for that is far better.*

Philippians 1:21, 23

*We would rather be away from the body
and at home with the Lord.*

2 Corinthians 5:8

The Bible does not view our bodies as bad. Christianity is not like some ancient Greek religions that treated the body as a burden to be gladly shed. No, death is an enemy. When our bodies die, we lose something precious. Christ is not against the body, but for the body. The Bible is clear on this: "The body is not meant for sexual immorality, but for the Lord, and the Lord for the body" (1 Corinthians 6:13). This is a wonderful statement: The Lord is for the body!

But we must not go so far as to say that without the body we can have no life and consciousness. The Bible does not teach this.

Christ died not only to redeem the body, but also to bind the soul so closely to himself that, even without the body, we are with him. This is a huge comfort in life and death, and Christ died so that we would enjoy this hope.

On the one hand the Bible talks about losing the body in death as a kind of nakedness for the soul: "While we are still in this tent [=the body], we groan . . . not that we would be unclothed, but that we would be further clothed" (2 Corinthians 5:4). In other words, we would rather move straight from here to the resurrection body with no in-between time when our bodies are in the grave. That's what those will experience who are alive when Christ returns from heaven.

But on the other hand, the Bible celebrates the in-between time, when our souls are in heaven and our bodies are in the grave. This is not the final glory, but it is glorious. We read, "To live is Christ, and to die is gain" (Philippians 1:21). "Gain"! Yes, loss of the body for a season. In a sense, "unclothed." But more than anything else, "gain"! Why? Because death for the Christian will mean coming home to Christ. As the apostle Paul says: "My desire is to depart and be with Christ, for that is far better" (Philippians 1:23).

"Far better"! Not yet in every way the best. That will come when the body is raised in health and glory. But still "far better." We will be with Christ in a way that is more intimate, more "at home." So the early Christians said, "We would rather be away from the body and at home with the Lord" (2 Corinthians 5:8). Those of us who believe in Christ do not go out of existence when we die. We do not go into a kind of "soul sleep." We go to be with Christ. We are "at home." It is "far better." It is "gain."

This is one of the great reasons Christ suffered. "[He] died for us so that whether we are awake or asleep we might live with him" (1 Thessalonians 5:10). Sleep-like, the body lies there in the grave. But we live with Christ in heaven. This is not our final hope. Someday the body will be raised. But short of that, to be with Christ is precious beyond words.

To Secure Our Resurrection
from the Dead

*For if we have been united with him in a death like his,
we shall certainly be united with him in a resurrection like his.*

Romans 6:5

*If the Spirit of him who raised Jesus from the dead dwells in you,
he who raised Christ Jesus from the dead will also give life to
your mortal bodies through his Spirit who dwells in you.*

Romans 8:11

*If we have died with him,
we will also live with him.*

2 Timothy 2:11

The keys of death were hung on the inside of Christ's tomb. From the outside, Christ could do many wonderful works, including raising a twelve-year-old girl and two men from the dead—only to die again (Mark 5:41-42; Luke 7:14-15; John 11:43-44). If any were to be raised from the dead, never to die again, Christ would have to die for them, enter the tomb, take the keys, and unlock the door of death from the inside.

The resurrection of Jesus is God's gift and proof that his death was completely successful in blotting out the sins of his people and removing the wrath of God. You can see this in the word "therefore." Christ was "obedient to the point of death, even death on a cross. *Therefore* God has highly exalted him"

(Philippians 2:8-9). From the cross the Son of God cried, "It is finished" (John 19:30). And by means of the resurrection, God the Father cries, "It was finished indeed!" The great work of paying for our sin and providing our righteousness and satisfying God's justice was finished in the death of Jesus.

Then, in the grave, he had the right and the power to take the keys of death and open the door for all who come to him by faith. If sin is paid for, and righteousness is provided, and justice is satisfied, nothing can keep Christ or his people in the grave. That's why Jesus shouts, "I died, and behold I am alive forevermore, and I have the keys of Death and Hades" (Revelation 1:18).

The Bible rings with the truth that belonging to Jesus means we will be raised from the dead with him. "If we have been united with him in a death like his, we shall certainly be united with him in a resurrection like his" (Romans 6:5). "Since we believe that Jesus died and rose again, even so, through Jesus, God will bring with him those who have fallen asleep" (1 Thessalonians 4:14). "God raised the Lord and will also raise us up by his power" (1 Corinthians 6:14).

Here's the connection between Christ's death and our resurrection: "The sting of death is sin, and the power of sin is the law" (1 Corinthians 15:56). Which means, we have all sinned, and the law sentences sinners to everlasting death. But the text continues, "Thanks be to God, who gives us the victory through our Lord Jesus Christ" (verse 57). In other words, the demand of the law is met by Jesus' life and death. Therefore, sins are forgiven. Therefore, the sting of sin is removed. Therefore, those who believe in Christ will *not* be sentenced to everlasting death, but will "be raised imperishable . . . then shall come to pass the saying that is written: 'Death is swallowed up in victory'" (1 Corinthians 15:52, 54). Be astonished, and come to Christ. He invites you: "I am the resurrection and the life. Whoever believes in me, though he die, yet shall he live" (John 11:25).

To Disarm the Rulers and Authorities

He set aside [the legal brief against us], nailing it to the cross.
He disarmed the rulers and authorities and put them
to open shame, by triumphing over them in him.

Colossians 2:14-15

The reason the Son of God appeared
was to destroy the works of the devil.

1 John 3:8

In the Bible, "rulers and authorities" can refer to human governments. But when we read that on the cross Christ "disarmed the rulers and authorities" and "put them to open shame" and "triumphed over them," we should think of the demonic powers that afflict the world. One of the clearest statements about these evil powers is Ephesians 6:12. It says that Christians "do not wrestle against flesh and blood, but against the *rulers*, against the *authorities*, against the cosmic powers over this present darkness, against the spiritual forces of evil in the heavenly places."

Three times Satan is called "the ruler of this world." Just as Jesus was coming to the last hour of his life he said, "Now is the judgment of this world; now will the ruler of this world be cast out" (John 12:31). The death of Jesus was the decisive defeat of "the ruler of this world"—the devil. And as Satan goes, so go all his fallen angels. All of them were dealt a decisive blow of defeat when Christ died.

Not that they were put out of existence. We wrestle with them even now. But they are a defeated foe. We know we have the final victory. It is as though a great dragon has had his head cut off and is thrashing about until he bleeds to death. The battle is won. But we must still be careful of the damage he can do.

In the death of Jesus, God was "canceling the record of debt that stood against us with its legal demands. This he set aside, nailing it to the cross" (Colossians 2:14; see chapter 7). This is how he "disarmed the rulers and authorities and put them to open shame." In other words, if God's law no longer condemns us, because Christ canceled our debt, then Satan has no grounds to accuse us.

Accusation of God's people was the devil's great work before Christ. The very word *Satan* means "adversary or accuser." But listen to what happened when Christ died. These are the words of John the apostle: "I heard a loud voice in heaven, saying, 'Now the salvation and the power and the kingdom of our God and the authority of his Christ have come, for *the accuser of our brothers* has been thrown down'" (Revelation 12:10). This is the defeat and the disarming of the rulers and authorities.

Now in Christ no accusations can stand against God's people. "Who shall bring any charge against God's elect? It is God who justifies" (Romans 8:33). Neither man nor Satan can make a charge stick. The legal case is closed. Christ is our righteousness. Our accuser is disarmed. If he tries to speak in the court of heaven, shame will cover his face. Oh, how bold and free we should be in this world as we seek to serve Christ and love people! There is no condemnation for those who are in Christ. Let us then turn away from the temptations of the devil. His promises are lies, and his power is stripped.

To Unleash the Power of God in the Gospel

The word of the cross is folly to those who are perishing,
but to us who are being saved it is the power of God.

1 Corinthians 1:18

I am not ashamed of the gospel, for it is
the power of God for salvation to everyone
who believes, to the Jew first and also to the Greek.

Romans 1:16

Gospel means good news. It's news before it's theology. News is the reporting that something significant has happened. *Good* news is the announcement that something has happened that will make people happy. The gospel is the best news, because what it reports can make people happy forever.

What the gospel reports is the death and resurrection of Christ. The apostle Paul makes the news quality of the gospel plain:

I would remind you . . . of the gospel . . . that Christ died for our sins in accordance with the Scriptures, that he was buried, that he was raised on the third day . . . and that he . . . appeared to more than five hundred brothers at one time, most of whom are still alive. (1 Corinthians 15:1-7)

The heart of the gospel is that "Christ died for our sins . . . was buried . . . was raised . . . and appeared to more than five hundred people." The fact that he says many of these witnesses are still alive shows how factual the gospel is. He meant that his readers could find some witnesses and query them. The gospel is news about facts. And the facts were testable. There were witnesses of Jesus' death, burial, and resurrection life.

The tragic thing is that, for many, this good news seems foolish. Paul said, "The word of the cross is folly to those who are perishing, but to us who are being saved it is the power of God" (1 Corinthians 1:18). This is the power that Christ died to unleash. "The gospel . . . is the power of God for salvation to everyone who believes" (Romans 1:16).

Why is the death of Christ not seen as good news by all? We must see it as true and good before we can believe it. So the question is: Why do some see it as true and good and others don't? One answer is given in 2 Corinthians 4:4, "The god of this world [Satan] has blinded the minds of the unbelievers, to keep them from seeing the light of the gospel of the glory of Christ." Besides that, sinful human nature itself is dead to true spiritual reality. "The natural person does not accept the things of the Spirit of God, for they are folly to him" (1 Corinthians 2:14).

If anyone is going to see the gospel as true and good, satanic blindness and natural deadness must be overcome by the power of God. This is why the Bible says that even though the gospel is foolishness to many, yet "to those who are called . . . Christ [is] the power of God and the wisdom of God" (1 Corinthians 1:24). This "calling" is the merciful act of God to remove natural deadness and satanic blindness, so that we see Christ as true and good. This merciful act is itself a blood-bought gift of Christ. Look to him, and pray that God would enable you to see and embrace the gospel of Christ.

To Destroy the Hostility Between Races

He . . . has broken down in his flesh the dividing wall of hostility
by abolishing the law of commandments and ordinances,
that he might create in himself one new man in place of the two,
so making peace, and might reconcile us both to God in one body
through the cross, thereby killing the hostility.

Ephesians 2:14-16

The suspicion, prejudice, and demeaning attitudes between Jews and Gentiles (non-Jews) in New Testament times was as serious as the racial, ethnic, and national hostilities in our day. One example of the antagonism is what happened in Antioch between Cephas (sometimes called Peter) and Paul. Paul recounts the story: "When Cephas came to Antioch, I opposed him to his face, because he stood condemned. For before certain men came from James, he was eating with the Gentiles; but when they came he drew back and separated himself, fearing the circumcision party" (Galatians 2:11-12).

Peter had been living in the freedom of Jesus Christ. In spite of the fact that he was a Jewish Christian, he was eating with non-Jewish Christians. The dividing wall had come down. The hostility had been overcome. This is what Christ died to achieve. But then some very conservative Jews came to Antioch. Cephas panicked. He feared their criticism. So he pulled back from his fellowship with Gentiles.

The apostle Paul saw this happening. What would he do? Serve the status quo? Keep peace between the visiting conservatives and the more free Christian Jews in Antioch? The key to Paul's behavior is found in these words: "I saw that their conduct was not in step with the truth of the gospel" (Galatians 2:14). This is a crucial statement. Racial and ethnic segregation is a gospel issue! Cephas' fear and withdrawal from fellowship across ethnic lines was "not in step with the truth of the gospel." Christ had died to tear down this wall. And Cephas was building it up again.

So Paul did not serve the status quo, and he did not maintain a gospel-denying peace. He confronted Cephas publicly. "I said to Cephas before them all, 'If you, though a Jew, live like a Gentile [non-Jew] and not like a Jew, how can you force the Gentiles to live like Jews?'" (Galatians 2:14). In other words, Cephas' withdrawal from fellowship with non-Jewish Christians communicated a deadly message: You must become like Jews to be fully acceptable. This was the very thing that Christ died to abolish.

Jesus died to create a whole new way for races to be reconciled. Ritual and race are not the ground of joyful togetherness. Christ is. He fulfilled the law perfectly. All the aspects of it that separated people ended in him—except one: the gospel of Jesus Christ. It is impossible to build a lasting unity among races by saying that all religions can come together as equally valid. Jesus Christ is the Son of God. God sent him into the world as the one and only means of saving sinners and reconciling races forever. If we deny this, we undermine the very foundation of eternal hope and everlasting unity among peoples. By his death on the cross, something cosmic, not parochial, was accomplished. God and man were reconciled. Only as the races find and enjoy this will they love and enjoy each other forever. In overcoming our alienation from God, Christ overcomes it between races.

To Ransom People from Every Tribe and Language and People and Nation

*Worthy are you to take the scroll and to open its seals,
for you were slain, and by your blood you ransomed people for God
from every tribe and language and people and nation.*

Revelation 5:9

The scene is heaven. The apostle John has been given a glimpse of the future in the hand of God. "I saw in the right hand of him who was seated on the throne a scroll . . . sealed with seven seals" (Revelation 5:1). Opening the scroll signifies the unfolding of world history in the future. John weeps that there seems to be no one to open the scroll. Then one of the heavenly beings says, "Weep no more; behold, the Lion of the tribe of Judah, the Root of David, has conquered, so that he can open the scroll" (5:5). This is a reference to Jesus Christ, the Messiah. He had conquered by his death and resurrection. Then John sees him: "I saw a Lamb standing, as though it had been slain" (5:6).

Then the heavenly beings around the throne fall down and worship Christ. They sing a new song. Amazingly, the song announces that it is the death of Christ that makes him worthy to open the scroll of history. The implication is that Christ's death was necessary to accomplish God's global purposes in history. "They sang a new song, saying, 'Worthy are you to take the scroll and to open its seals, for you were slain, and by your blood you ransomed people for God from every tribe and language and people and nation'" (5:9).

Christ died to save a great diversity of peoples. Sin is no respecter of cultures. All peoples have sinned. Every race and culture needs to be reconciled to God. As the disease of sin is global, so the remedy is global. Jesus saw the agony of the cross coming and spoke boldly about the scope of his purpose: "I, when I am lifted up from the earth, will draw all people to myself" (John 12:32). As he planned his death, he embraced the world.

Christianity began in the East. Over the centuries there was a major shift to the West. But increasingly now, Christianity is not a Western religion. This is no surprise to Christ. Already in the Old Testament his global impact was foretold: "All the ends of the earth shall remember and turn to the LORD, and all the families of the nations shall worship before you" (Psalm 22:27). "Let the nations be glad and sing for joy" (Psalm 67:4). So when Jesus came to the end of his ministry on earth, he made his mission clear: "that the Christ should suffer and on the third day rise from the dead, and that repentance and forgiveness of sins should be proclaimed in his name *to all nations*" (Luke 24:46-47). The command to his disciples was unmistakable: "Go therefore and make disciples of *all nations*" (Matthew 28:19).

Jesus Christ is not a tribal deity. He does not belong to one culture or one ethnic group. He is "the Lamb of God, who takes away the sin of the world" (John 1:29). "There is no distinction between Jew and Greek [or any other group]; the same Lord is Lord of all, bestowing his riches on all who call on him. For 'everyone who calls on the name of the Lord will be saved'" (Romans 10:12-13). Call on him now, and join the great global band of the redeemed.

To Gather All His Sheep
from Around the World

[Caiaphas] did not say this of his own accord,
but being high priest that year he prophesied
that Jesus would die for the nation, and not for the nation only,
but also to gather into one the children of God
who are scattered abroad.

John 11:51-52

And I have other sheep that are not of this fold.
I must bring them also, and they will listen to my voice.
So there will be one flock, one shepherd.

John 10:16

Without knowing it, a donkey may speak for God (Numbers 22:28). So may a preacher or a priest. It happened to Caiaphas, who was the high priest in Israel when Jesus was being tried for his life. Unwittingly he said to the leaders of Israel, "It is better for you that one man should die for the people, not that the whole nation should perish" (John 11:50). This had a double meaning. Caiaphas meant: Better that Jesus die than that the Romans accuse the nation of treason and destroy the people. But God had another meaning. So the Bible says, "[Caiaphas] did not say this of his own accord, but being high priest that year he prophesied that Jesus would die for the nation, and not for the nation only, but also to gather into one the children of God who are scattered abroad" (John 11:51-52).

Jesus himself said the same thing with a different metaphor. Instead of "children . . . scattered abroad," Jesus spoke of "sheep" outside the fold of Israel: "I have other sheep that are not of this fold. I must bring them also, and they will listen to my voice. So there will be one flock, one shepherd" (John 10:16).

Both of these ways of saying it are astonishing. They teach that all over the world there are people whom God has chosen to be reached and saved by Jesus Christ. There are "children of God . . . scattered abroad." There are "sheep not of this [Jewish] fold." This means that God is very aggressive in gathering a people for his Son. He calls his people to go make disciples, but he also goes before them. He has a people chosen before his messengers get there. So Jesus speaks of converts whom God had made his own and then brought to Christ. "All that the Father gives me will come to me, and whoever comes to me I will never cast out. . . . Yours they were, and you gave them to me" (John 6:37; 17:6).

It is an awesome thing that God looks down on all the peoples of the world and names a flock for himself, and then sends missionaries in the name of Christ, and then leads his chosen ones to the sound of the gospel, and then saves them. They could be saved no other way. Missions is essential. "The sheep hear his voice, and he calls his own sheep by name and leads them out . . . the sheep follow him, for they know his voice" (John 10:3-4).

Jesus suffered and died so that the sheep could hear his voice and live. That's what Caiaphas said without knowing it: "Jesus would die . . . not for the nation only, but also to gather into one the children of God who are scattered abroad." He gave up his life to gather the sheep. By his blood he bought the mercy that makes his voice unmistakable to his own. Pray that God would apply that mercy to you, and that you would hear and live.

To Rescue Us from Final Judgment

Christ, having been offered once to bear the sins of many,
will appear a second time, not to deal with sin
but to save those who are eagerly waiting for him.

Hebrews 9:28

The Christian idea of salvation relates to past, present, and future. The Bible says, "By grace you *have been saved* through faith" (Ephesians 2:8). It says that the gospel is the power of God "to us who are *being saved*" (1 Corinthians 1:18). And it says, "*Salvation is nearer to us now* than when we first believed" (Romans 13:11). We have been saved. We are being saved. We will be saved.

At every stage we are saved by the death of Christ. In the past, once for all, our sins were paid for by Christ himself. We were justified by faith alone. In the present, the death of Christ secures the power of God's Spirit to save us progressively from the domination and contamination of sin. And in the future, it will be the blood of Christ, poured out on the cross, that protects us from the wrath of God and brings us to perfection and joy.

There is a real judgment coming. The Bible describes "a fearful expectation of judgment, and a fury of fire that will consume the adversaries" (Hebrews 10:27). It calls us to live "with reverence and awe, for our God is a consuming fire" (Hebrews 12:28-29).

Jesus warned the people of his day to "flee from the wrath to come" (Matthew 3:7). For Jesus himself will be "revealed from heaven with his mighty angels in flaming fire, inflicting vengeance on those who do not know God and on those who do not obey the gospel of our Lord Jesus. They will suffer the punishment of eternal destruction, away from the presence of the Lord and from the glory of his might" (2 Thessalonians 1:7-9).

Some pictures of this final wrath of God are almost too terrible to ponder. Ironically, it is John, the "apostle of love," who gives us the most graphic glimpses of hell. Those who reject Christ and give their allegiance to another "will drink the wine of God's wrath, poured full strength into the cup of his anger, and . . . will be tormented with fire and sulfur in the presence of the holy angels and in the presence of the Lamb. And the smoke of their torment goes up forever and ever, and they have no rest, day or night" (Revelation 14:10-11).

Until we feel some measure of dread about God's future wrath, we will probably not grasp the sweetness with which the early church savored the saving work of Christ in the future: "[We] wait for his Son from heaven, whom he raised from the dead, Jesus who delivers us from the wrath to come" (1 Thessalonians 1:10). Jesus Christ, and he alone, can save us from the wrath to come. Without him, we will be swept away forever.

But when he saves us in the end, it will be on the basis of his blood. "Christ, having been offered once to bear the sins of many, will appear a second time, not to deal with sin but to save those who are eagerly waiting for him" (Hebrews 9:28). Sin was dealt with once for all. No new sacrifice is needed. Our shield from future wrath is as sure as the sufferings of Christ in our place. For the sake of the cross, then, exult in future grace.

To Gain His Joy and Ours

For the joy that was set before him,
[he] endured the cross, despising the shame,
and is seated at the right hand of the throne of God.

Hebrews 12:2

The path that leads to joy is a hard road. It's hard for us, and it was hard for Jesus. It cost him his life. It may cost us ours. "For the joy that was set before him [he] endured the cross." First the agony of the cross, then the ecstasy of heaven. There was no other way.

The joy set before him had many levels. It was the joy of reunion with his Father: "In your presence there is fullness of joy; at your right hand are pleasures forevermore" (Psalm 16:11). It was the joy of triumph over sin: "After making purification for sins, he sat down at the right hand of the Majesty on high" (Hebrews 1:3). It was the joy of divine rights restored: "[He] is seated at the right hand of the throne of God" (Hebrews 12:2). It was the joy of being surrounded with praise by all the people for whom he died: "There will be . . . joy in heaven over one sinner who repents"—not to mention millions (Luke 15:7).

Now what about us? Has he entered into joy and left us for misery? No. Before he died, he made the connection between his joy and ours. He said, "These things I have spoken to you, that my joy may be in you, and that your joy may be full" (John 15:11). He knew what his joy would be, and he said, "My joy will be in you." We who have trusted in him will rejoice with as much of the joy of Jesus as finite creatures can experience.

But the road will be hard. Jesus warned us, "In the world you will have tribulation" (John 16:33). "A disciple is not above his teacher. . . . If they have called the master of the house Beelzebul, how much more will they malign those of his household" (Matthew 10:24-25). "Some of you they will put to death. You will be hated by all for my name's sake" (Luke 21:16-17). That's the path Jesus walked, and that's the road to joy—his joy triumphant in us, and our joy full.

In the same way that the hope of joy enabled Christ to endure the cross, our hope of joy empowers us to suffer with him. Jesus prepared us for this very thing when he said, "Blessed are you when others revile you and persecute you and utter all kinds of evil against you falsely on my account. Rejoice and be glad, for your reward is great in heaven" (Matthew 5:11-12). Our reward will be to enjoy God with the very joy that the Son of God has in his Father.

If Jesus had not willingly died, neither he nor we could be forever glad. He would have been disobedient. We would have perished in our sins. His joy and ours were acquired at the cross. Now we follow him in the path of love. We reckon "that the sufferings of this present time are not worth comparing with the glory that is to be revealed to us" (Romans 8:18). Now we bear reproach with him. But then there will be undiminished joy. Any risk required by love we will endure. Not with heroic might, but in the strength of hope that "Weeping may tarry for the night, but joy comes with the morning" (Psalm 30:5).

So That He Would Be Crowned with Glory and Honor

But we see . . . Jesus, crowned with glory and honor
because of the suffering of death.

Hebrews 2:9

And being found in human form, he humbled himself
by becoming obedient to the point of death, even death on a cross.
Therefore God has highly exalted him and bestowed on him
the name that is above every name.

Philippians 2:7-9

Worthy is the Lamb who was slain,
to receive power and wealth and wisdom
and might and honor and glory and blessing!

Revelation 5:12

The night before he died, knowing what was coming, Jesus prayed, "Father, glorify me in your own presence with the glory that I had with you before the world existed" (John 17:5). And so it came to pass: He was "crowned with glory and honor *because of* the suffering of death" (Hebrews 2:9). His glory was the reward of his suffering. He was "obedient to the point of death. . . . *Therefore* God has highly exalted him" (Philippians 2:8-9). Precisely *because* he was slain, the Lamb is "worthy . . . to receive . . . honor and glory" (Revelation 5:12). The passion of

Jesus Christ did not merely precede the crown; it was the price, and the crown was the prize. He died to have it.

Many people stumble at this point. They say, "How can this be loving? How can Jesus be motivated to give us joy if he is motivated to get his glory? Since when is vanity a virtue?" That is a good question, and it has a wonderful biblical answer.

The answer lies in learning what great love really is. Most of us have grown up thinking that being loved means being made much of. Our whole world seems to be built on this assumption. If I love you, I make much of you. I help you feel good about yourself. It is as though a sight of the self is the secret of joy.

But we know better. Even before we come to the Bible, we know this is not so. Our happiest moments have not been self-saturated moments, but self-forgetful moments. There have been times when we stood beside the Grand Canyon, or at the foot of Mount Kilimanjaro, or viewed a stunning sunset over the Sahara, and for a fleeting moment felt the joy of sheer wonder. This is what we were made for. Paradise will not be a hall of mirrors. It will be a display of majesty. And it won't be ours.

If this is true, and if Christ is the most majestic reality in the universe, then what must his love to us be? Surely not making much of us. That would not satisfy our souls. We were made for something much greater. If we are to be as happy as we can be, we must see and savor the most glorious person of all, Jesus Christ himself. This means that to love us, Jesus must seek the fullness of his glory and offer it to us for our enjoyment. That is why he prayed, the night before he died, "Father, I desire that they also, whom you have given me, may be with me where I am, to see my glory" (John 17:24). That was love. "I will show them my glory." When Jesus died to regain the fullness of his glory, he died for our joy. Love is the labor—whatever the cost—of helping people be enthralled with what will satisfy them most, namely, Jesus Christ. That is how Jesus loves.

TO SHOW THAT THE WORST EVIL IS MEANT BY GOD FOR GOOD

*In this city there were gathered together
against your holy servant Jesus . . . both Herod and Pontius Pilate,
along with the Gentiles and the peoples of Israel, to do
whatever your hand and your plan
had predestined to take place.*

Acts 4:27-28

The most profound thing we can say about suffering and evil is that, in Jesus Christ, God entered into it and turned it for good. The origin of evil is shrouded in mystery. The Bible does not take us as far as we might like to go. Rather it says, "The secret things belong to . . . God" (Deuteronomy 29:29).

The heart of the Bible is not an explanation of where evil came from, but a demonstration of how God enters into it and turns it for the very opposite—everlasting righteousness and joy. There were pointers in the Scriptures all along the way that it would be like this for the Messiah. Joseph, the son of Jacob, was sold into slavery in Egypt. He seemed abandoned for seventeen years. But God was in it and made him ruler in Egypt, so that in a great famine he could save the very ones who sold him. The story is summed up in a word from Joseph to his brothers: "As for you,

you meant evil against me, but God meant it for good" (Genesis 50:20). A foreshadowing of Jesus Christ, forsaken in order to save.

Or consider Christ's ancestry. Once God was the only king in Israel. But the people rebelled and asked for a human king: "No! But there shall be a king over us" (1 Samuel 8:19). Later they confessed, "We have added to all our sins this evil, to ask for ourselves a king" (1 Samuel 12:19). But God was in it. From the line of these kings he brought Christ into the world. The sinless Savior had his earthly origin in sin as he came to save sinners.

But the most astonishing thing is that evil and suffering were Christ's appointed way of victory over evil and suffering. Every act of treachery and brutality against Jesus was sinful and evil. But God was in it. The Bible says, "Jesus [was] delivered up [to death] according to the definite plan and foreknowledge of God" (Acts 2:23). The lash on his back, the thorns on his head, the spit on his cheek, the bruises on his face, the nails in his hands, the spear in his side, the scorn of rulers, the betrayal of his friend, the desertion by his disciples—these were all the result of sin, and all designed by God to destroy the power of sin. "Herod and Pontius Pilate, along with the Gentiles and the peoples of Israel, [did] whatever your hand and your plan had predestined to take place" (Acts 4:27-28).

There is no greater sin than to hate and kill the Son of God. There was no greater suffering nor any greater innocence than the suffering and innocence of Christ. Yet God was in it all. "It was the will of the LORD to crush him" (Isaiah 53:10). His aim, through evil and suffering, was to destroy evil and suffering. "With his stripes we are healed" (Isaiah 53:5). Is not then the passion of Jesus Christ meant by God to show the world that there is no sin and no evil too great that God, in Christ, cannot bring from it everlasting righteousness and joy? The very suffering that we caused became the hope of our salvation. "Father, forgive them, for they know not what they do" (Luke 23:34).

A PRAYER

Father in heaven, in the name of Jesus Christ, I ask for every reader that you would confirm what is true in this book, and cancel out what may be false. I pray that no one would stumble over Christ or take offense at his deity, or at his unparalleled suffering, or at the purposes of his passion. For many, these things are new. May they be patient to consider them carefully. And would you grant understanding and insight.

I pray that the fog of indifference to eternal things would be lifted, and that the reality of heaven and hell would become clear. I pray that the centrality of Christ in history would become plain, and that his passion would be seen as the most important event that ever happened. Grant us to walk along the cliff of eternity, where the wind blows crystal-clear with truth.

And I pray that our attention would not be deflected from the supremacy of your own divine purposes in Christ's passion. Forbid that we would be consumed by the lesser question that asks which people killed your Son. All of us were involved, because of our sin. But that is not the main issue. *Your* design and *your* act are the main issues. O Lord, open our eyes to see that you yourself, and no man, planned the passion of Jesus Christ. And from this awesome position, let us look out over the endless panorama of your merciful, hope-filled purposes in the passion of Christ.

What an amazing truth you have revealed: "Christ Jesus came into the world to save sinners" (1 Timothy 1:15). He did it not mainly by his teaching, but by his dying. "Christ died for our sins in accordance with the Scriptures" (1 Corinthians 15:3). Is there any more wonderful message for people like us, who know we cannot measure up to the demands of our own conscience, let alone the demands of your own holiness?

Would you, then, merciful Father, grant that all who read this book would see their need, and see your perfect provision in Christ, and believe. I pray this because of the promise of your Son: "For God so loved the world, that he gave his only Son, that whoever believes in him should not perish but have eternal life" (John 3:16). In Jesus' merciful name, I pray, amen.

BOOKS ON THE HISTORICAL RELIABILITY OF THE BIBLE'S RECORD

*I*f you want to read some of the best scholarship on the life, death, and resurrection of Jesus, I would recommend the following books.

Blomberg, Craig L. *The Historical Reliability of the Gospels.* Downers Grove, Ill.: InterVarsity Press, 1987.

Copan, Paul, ed. *Will the Real Jesus Please Stand Up? A Debate Between William Lane Craig and John Dominic Crossan.* Grand Rapids, Mich.: Baker, 1999.

Craig, William Lane, ed. *Jesus' Resurrection: Fact or Figment? A Debate Between William Lane Craig and Gerd Ludemann.* Downers Grove, Ill.: InterVarsity Press, 2000.

Craig, William Lane. *The Son Rises: The Historical Evidence for the Resurrection of Jesus.* Eugene, Ore.: Wipf & Stock, 2001.

Habermas, Gary R. *The Historical Jesus: Ancient Evidence for the Life of Christ.* Joplin, Mo.: College Press, 1996.

Wilkins, Michael J. and J. P. Moreland, eds. *Jesus Under Fire: Modern Scholarship Reinvents the Historical Jesus.* Grand Rapids, Mich.: Zondervan, 1996.

NOTES

1. Elie Wiesel, *Night* (New York: Bantam Books, 1982, orig. 1960), p. 72.
2. Ibid., p. 73.
3. Ibid., p. 32.
4. John Newton, "Come, My Soul, Thy Suit Prepare," in *The Trinity Hymnal* (Philadelphia: Great Commission Publications, 1962), p. 531.

Desiring God Ministries exists to help you say—from the heart—that "to live is Christ and to die is gain" (Philippians 1:21). Nothing would make us happier than for you to finish reading this book and say: "Far be it from me to boast except in the cross of our Lord Jesus Christ, by which the world has been crucified to me, and I to the world" (Galatians 6:14).

If God has used this book to show you his glory and beauty in the suffering and death of Jesus Christ, we'd love to know about it. And if there is anything we can do to help you know him more, we'd love to help.

For over twenty years John Piper has been preaching sermons at Bethlehem Baptist Church. All of the manuscripts are online for free at our website: *www.desiringGOD.org*. New, free, down-loadable, MP3 audio sermons are posted to the site each week. You can read articles about dozens of topics and see answers to frequently asked questions. You can be updated on upcoming conferences that we host. There's also a store where you can buy books, audio collections, and curriculum for children. Please don't let money be a barrier—we have a *whatever-you-can-afford*